43/35   M.

14 75

JAZZ MASTERS
OF THE
THIRTIES

A Da Capo Press Reprint Series

THE ROOTS OF JAZZ

JAZZ MASTERS
OF THE
THIRTIES

by Rex Stewart

Da Capo Press · New York · 1980

Library of Congress Cataloging in Publication Data

Stewart, Rex William, 1907-1967.
  Jazz masters of the thirties.

  (The Roots of jazz)
  Reprint of the ed. published by Macmillan Co., New
York, in series: The Macmillan jazz masters series.
    1. Jazz music. 2. Jazz musicians—Biography.
I. Title.
[ML3506.S84 1980]   785.42′092′2 [B]   79-27879
ISBN 0-306-76030-4

This Da Capo Press edition of
Jazz Masters of the Thirties
is an unabridged republication of the
first edition published in New York
in 1972. It is reprinted by arrangement
with the Macmillan Publishing Co., Inc.

Published by Da Capo Press, Inc.
A Subsidiary of Plenum Publishing Corporation
227 West 17th Street, New York, N.Y. 10011

JAZZ MASTERS
OF THE
THIRTIES

JAZZ MASTERS
OF THE
THIRTIES

by Rex Stewart

MACMILLAN PUBLISHING CO., INC.
NEW YORK
COLLIER MACMILLAN PUBLISHERS
LONDON

MACMILLAN PUBLISHING CO., INC.

866 THIRD AVENUE, NEW YORK, N.Y. 10022

COLLIER-MACMILLAN CANADA LTD.

TORONTO, ONTARIO

LIBRARY OF CONGRESS CATALOG CARD NUMBER: 73–169239

Second Printing 1973

PRINTED IN THE UNITED STATES OF AMERICA

Contents

Foreword

THE VOLUME WHICH FOLLOWS is unique in the literature of jazz. It is, as far as I know, the only published jazz history written by a musician that is not directly autobiographical.

As a musician, Rex Stewart writes with particular authority. But as an important contributor to the music of an era as well, he writes with unique personal and musical insight. He raises questions that only a jazz musician would raise; he deals with the music as only a participant could deal with it; and he writes of the lives of his fellow musicians as only a man named Rex Stewart could write of them. But a writer also has to deal with his readers, and that is a problem which Stewart, who took up writing only late in his life, well understood.

This is, of course, a posthumous book and as such has some limitations. I am sure that had Rex Stewart lived to prepare this collection for publication there would be more here on Teddy Wilson, Lionel Hampton, and Roy Eldridge; that men like Benny Goodman, Johnny Hodges, Count Basie, Lester Young, and others would enter here more than peripherally.

On the other hand, we have included material which takes us back to the 1920s, not only because it is valuable in itself but also because it sets the stage and provides a perspective on what follows.

I herewith offer thanks to several publications in which these chapters originally appeared: to *Down Beat* and its editors Don DeMicheal (who was in charge when these pieces began appearing) and Dan Morgenstern (who succeeded him); to *Evergreen Review;* and to the editors of the British *Music Maker* and *Melody Maker.*

Finally, a word on the two essays appended to this book. Special thanks go to Francis Thorne for his generosity in letting us include his biographical tribute to Rex Stewart, which originally appeared in the Italian magazine *Jazz di ieri e di Oggi.* And Hsio Wen Shih's chapter on Count Basie was to have been a part of *Jazz Masters of the Swing Era* as it was planned in the early 1960s.

MARTIN WILLIAMS

The Jean Goldkette Band

MOST PEOPLE seem to have forgotten that the first large white swinging orchestra was Jean Goldkette's. This band hit Roseland Ballroom on Manhattan's Gay White Way in 1927 like a tempestuous, tropical storm.

It opened the first set with a most unorthodox march version of *Valencia.* And when the sophisticated audience recognized the opening bars of a march tempo, they turned to each other in critical disbelief, only to break out into cheers before the number had finished.

We in the Fletcher Henderson Band were amazed, angry, morose, and bewildered as we sat on the opposite bandstand waiting our turn to go on—and it was a long wait—about forty-five minutes (the customary set was a half-hour)—because everything this band played prompted calls for encores from the crowd. This proved to be a most humiliating experience for us, since, after all, we were supposed to be the world's greatest dance orchestra. And up pops this Johnny-come-lately white band from out in the sticks, cutting us. Of course, we made excuses for ourselves, saying things like, "This wouldn't happen if Don Redman were here to lead the sax section." (Don, our first sax man, had stopped off in West Virginia to visit his folks.) But in our hearts, we knew that this was not really true. The facts were that we simply could not compete with Jean Goldkette's Victor Recording Orchestra.

Their arrangements were too imaginative and their rhythm too strong, what with Steve Brown slapping hell out of that bass fiddle and Frankie Trumbauer's inspiring leadership as he stood in front wailing on his C-melody saxophone. There was also the psychological advantage of having the crowd with them, since they were new faces and blowing like mad.

The first encounter with Goldkette's band should not have come as a surprise to us because we'd been forewarned. Charlie Horvath and Charlie Stanton at the Greystone Ballroom in Detroit had said that we'd get cut when we met the Victor band, but this did not mean a thing to us. They had also complimented Smack's band on the way we'd broken the house up with our stomping, swinging playing, and we didn't need them to tell us how great we were. We felt that we had a champion outfit, and justifiably so, since according to audiences everywhere we had played on the tour, we were kings of the road. But that engagement at Roseland proved Stanton and Horvath, oh, so right. We learned that Jean Goldkette's orchestra was, without any question, the greatest in the world and the first original white swing band in jazz history.

Before proceeding, let me fill what I feel is a large gap in music history. There's been relatively little mention of Goldkette, which brings to mind the irony contained in a statement attributed to Eddie Condon, who allegedly said something like this about a French critic: "We don't tell Frenchmen how to jump on grapes, so what makes them think they can tell us anything about jazz?"

Such an observation might have been true and valid up to a certain point, but circumstances do alter cases. There is, and was, such an exception in the case of Jean Goldkette, a Frenchman, who not only told us about jazz but also dedicated his life to sponsoring and creating jazz, thereby showing us Americans a lot about the music.

Jean arrived in this country in 1911, when he was twelve. Though born in France, he had been reared in Greece, where he started his training as a classical pianist. Then he continued his studies in Russia. I am told that some relatives in Chicago encouraged him to come here, feeling that this country afforded greater outlet for his talents. On his arrival, Jean soon found out that those cold breezes that swept into the city off Lake Michigan were mild compared with his reception as a concert pianist. This state of affairs finally led Goldkette into the dance-band business, and here he found his niche, fitting right in with the type of music that was current—waltzes, polkas, schottisches, and, once in a while, a clumsy version of that daring new dance, the foxtrot. Starting with one of the lesser-known groups, Jean quickly established a reputation and came to the attention of Mr. Big, Edgar Benson, whose orchestras were the toast of Chicago. Goldkette did so well as a subleader that Benson later sent him to Detroit to head the Benson orchestra there. But this took place quite a while after Jean had found out about the wild wonderful music that could be heard on Chicago's south side. There the atmosphere was highlighted by the symphonic ragtime arrangements of Doc Cook's large orchestra (eighteen men), which played nightly at Paddy Harmon's White City Amusement Park, captivating Chicagoans during those times. On the other end of the musical spectrum, there was King Joe Oliver, Jimmie Noone, Jasper Taylor, and a lot of other talented tooters who were playing it sweet and lowdown all night long, to the delight of Goldkette and other music lovers.

The stimulating feelings that came from this free-style improvisation remained with Jean for the rest of his life and certainly were reflected in his later efforts. Jean tried very hard to play like his south-side heroes, but the style was not for his piano, and he never did become good as a jazz pianist. But he did wind up playing dance music, which he must have done quite creditably, for Benson tapped him for Detroit. The first big job of record that he played, as leader of a Benson unit, was at the elegant Detroit Athletic Club. At first, however, his orchestra attracted no more attention among the hoity-toity audience than the ornate cuspidors. Inexplicably at some later society event, most of the staid dowagers and their equally conservative spouses left the club earlier than usual. Jean, perhaps in desperation, let his hair down, and the band played some toe-tapping dance music. Ears perked up, and the floor quickly became crowded as the younger set got the message. They ate up the ragtime and applauded for more. This acceptance did not go unnoticed by the management, because more and more of the sons and daughters of their wealthy clientele began to frequent the spot.

In those days, the Benson orchestra was le plus ultra of society dance music. This was the early twenties, just about the time when the new millionaires of the Motor City were avidly going through the motions of acquiring culture.

Civic pride combined with this opulence to produce a hotel of splendor and stature, comparable to New York's and Chicago's finest. It was first called the Book Hotel, later the Book-Cadillac. With the accoutrements first class, it followed that the hotel had to have the best music available. So the management turned to Benson himself in Chicago. Benson, although flattered by the amount of money offered, did not choose to leave his green pastures in the Windy City and proposed his Jean Goldkette group for the engagement. As far as Detroit was concerned, the rest is history. Goldkette came, was heard, and became *the* name there.

From that start, Goldkette was established, and his groups played both the Book-Cadillac Hotel and the Detroit Athletic Club for years. Jean's fame came to far surpass that of Benson, and he could very well have sat back on his laurels as a midwestern counterpart of Meyer Davis. He had more engagements than he could handle. But this was not the nature of the man. He continued to branch out, possibly because of his love for musicians and his feeling for jazz.

Between 1922 and 1923, an organization of Chinese started building a huge restaurant. For some reason, they were unable to complete it, and it became available for sale. Jean, on learning about the property from banker friends, was able to obtain financing enough to lease the building—and the Greystone Ballroom was born.

Now Goldkette was in a position to do all the things he'd dreamed of doing. With the contracts for providing the music at the Detroit Athletic Club and the Book-Cadillac in his pocket as a backstop, he was in business. Bolstered by his belief in jazz, he felt that the acquisition would do two things—give him an outlet so that he could cater to the tastes of the little people, and he also could now hire those red-hot tooters, most of whom were only names to him. The list of talent is too long to repeat in toto, but there is no question in my mind that some of the greatest names in the business at one time or another worked under Goldkette's banner.

He was a pioneer in the big-band field, and during his life he created several orchestras, built many ballrooms, and operated throughout the Midwest on such a large scale that eventually he became the most important impresario in the area bounded by Buffalo, Chicago, Toronto, and New Orleans. Society vied for his music, and hoi poloi thronged to his ballrooms nightly. No horse show, fete, or upper-crust event really was "in" without the stamp of Goldkette music.

Among the many musical organizations he formed were the Casa Loma Band, the Studebaker Champions, the Orange Blossoms under the direction of Hank Begnini, the Detroit Athletic Club Orchestra under the leadership of Owen Bartlett, and the Book-Cadillac orchestra led by Paul Mertz. Goldkette took over management of many other bands that were in operation already, such as McKinney's Cotton Pickers.

Meanwhile, he had an empire of ballrooms and owned or operated places in Toronto, Indiana, Ohio, Detroit, and several resort spots on the Great Lakes. He'd conceive an idea and then turn over the execution of it to Charlie Horvath, his second in command.

There's quite a story about how Horvath rose to the position of major domo in the Goldkette enterprises. It seems that Jean had known the Horvath family in Europe during the period when their string ensemble was considered one of the foremost on the Continent. When Goldkette went to the Motor City, there was a grand reunion with Papa Horvath, who by that time was in the Detroit Symphony Orchestra.

Charlie and Jean quickly joined forces. Charlie had taken up drums and later held down the percussion spot with the Goldkette band. The close ties developed into the team of Goldkette and Horvath.

There are some who say that Charlie was the brains behind the association. For all I know, this may well be true. When they broke up, Charlie moved on to Cleveland, where he operated his own ballroom. Jean's fortunes went into decline while Horvath prospered.

The Goldkette Victor band was the first and greatest white swing band. There can be no doubt that this is true. The personnel varied from time to time, since Goldkette was a great one for switching musicians around when he felt that a particular talent fit a special situation.

According to Mertz, who played piano in most of Jean's orchestras, he no sooner would get settled at a resort or perhaps at the Book-Cadillac than Jean would telephone, saying, "Paul, get out to Kansas City" or down to the ballroom in Indiana.

No other white orchestra boasted such an array of skilled jazzmen at one time as did Jean Goldkette's. Not even Paul Whiteman (who hired many of Goldkette's former stars after the group disbanded) was able to bring about such swinging or such esprit de corps, principally because the freewheeling joy of playing with one another had vanished—this, even though Whiteman had the true sparkplugs of the Victor organization with him in Frankie Trumbauer and Bix Beiderbecke. But even they were seldom able to get the Whiteman aggregation off the ground.

Aside from such giants as Tram and Bix, who received accolades that carry over to today, there were many others who, if they were not quite in the same league, certainly were on a par with the best players at that time. I am speaking of fellows like Don Murray, Fud Livingston, Jimmy Dorsey, Danny Polo—the clarinet players. The trombone men were Russ Morgan, Tommy Dorsey, Miff Mole, Bill Rank, Speigan Wilcox, and for trumpets, Fuzzy Farar, Sterling Bose, Red Nichols, Ray Lodwig. There were also violinist Joe Venuti, guitarist Eddie Lang, drummer Chauncey Morehouse, and several more.

One of the great mysteries, as far as I am concerned, is why so little had been written about this most important white swing band.

You can believe me that the Goldkette band was the original predecessor to any large white dance orchestra that followed, up to Benny Goodman. Even Goodman, swinger that he was, did not come close to the tremendous sound of Goldkette or the inventive arrangements of the Goldkette repertoire, not in quality and certainly not in quantity. Of this I am positive, because I was in Fletcher's band when that memorable confrontation took place at Roseland.

Perhaps one reason this organization has never been given the recognition that it should have is that it came along before most of the present-day chroniclers knew beans about the music or the men who made it. Another reason is that when Goldkette had the cream of the crop playing in his bands, recording was in its infancy and reproduction at that time did not project anything like the real performances. So, naturally, the Goldkette recordings did not reflect the verve and consummate artistry of the ensemble.

The Goldkette group began recording in 1924, and the personnel is a bit uncertain but may have included some or all of the following: Fuzzy Farrar, Red Nichols, Paul Van Loan, George Crozier, Don Murray, Joe Venuti, Bill Kreutz, and Charlie Horvath. They made such hits as *Eileen, Honest and Truly, Remember,* and *What's the Use of Dreaming?*

Among the personnel in 1926 were Fud Livingston, Eddie Lang, Itzy Riskin, Steve Brown (aside from many of the others from the 1924 dates). Arrangements were by Russ Morgan. This band recorded *After I Say I'm Sorry; Dinah; Gimme a Little Kiss, Will Ya, Huh?; Lonesome and Sorry,* and many other big songs of the day. Beiderbecke and Trumbauer recorded with the band later that year, and in 1927 the Dorsey brothers were added for recordings. The period between 1926 and 1929 was the heyday of the band, because by that time they had a huge writing staff consisting of Paul Mertz, Russ Morgan, Bill Challis, and Joe Glover.

Too, many of the young musicians who had joined Goldkette grew to tremendous stature under his aegis. Venuti was the premier jazz violinist of the day, and his sidekick, Lang, was father of the jazz guitar. (A little-known fact is that Lang was the inspiration for the great gypsy guitarist, Django Reinhardt—or so Django told me.) Then there was Murray, one of the greatest clarinetists who ever lived. Brown brought the art of slapping the bass fiddle direct from New Orleans, where he had heard the Negroes do it.

The artistry of Trumbauer on the C-melody saxophone made a lady of the instrument. By playing it so well, he inspired some players but discouraged many others, who realized that they could never compete with his genius and so gave up the instrument. It subsequently went out of fashion. I am only speculating that Trumbauer was responsible for this, but the fact is that after Tram, little was heard on the horn again.

Perhaps greatest of all the luminaries was Beiderbecke. I felt very close to him, for we shared the same locker at Roseland (everybody had to double up with lockers), and we would hang out together at the speakeasy in the same building. Many is the time we had our own private session in the band room after Broadway had settled down for the evening. Admiring Bix as I did, it was not difficult for me to attempt to copy his memorable solo on *Singing the Blues,* especially since the phonograph company for which Fletcher recorded the number wanted my solo as close to the original as possible.

As a matter of fact, there was a lot of copying going on. It was a mutual admiration society, with Fletcher and Goldkette exchanging arrangements, which stood Fletcher's band in good stead later. We carved the Casa Loma Band (a Goldkette outfit) at the Penn Athletic Club in Philadephia using Goldkette's arrangements!

In my book Bix was a once-in-a-million artist. I doubt if what he played will ever be surpassed on the trumpet. He was one of the all-time giants, and I feel that his gifts remain today as unsullied and strikingly refreshing as when he lived.

Unfortunately, the same cannot be said for Goldkette. Most of what he was is both forgotten and unrecognized. I can only hope that this brief recounting will help to keep his memory alive.

Down Beat, April 20, 1967

Smack! Memories of
Fletcher Henderson

TODAY'S JAZZ LISTENER is likely to be unaware of the huge debt that current music owes to James Fletcher Henderson. Ragtime, swing, bop, and Third Stream all stem from the same tree. Fashions in music happen and change with such speed that it becomes increasingly difficult to realize what an infant jazz still is, in comparison with other art forms.

Further, there exists an explainable—but notwithstanding, total —lack of communication between our current favorites—Charlie Mingus, John Coltrane, Thelonious Monk, Miles Davis, and Neophonic jazz—and what has gone on before—Jelly Roll Morton, Willard Robison, Bix Beiderbecke, etc.—which makes this contemporary scene possible.

Fletcher Henderson was a bridge between the earliest forms and what later evolved. I consider myself blessed to have been there and a part of the action in the twenties in New York, when musical history was being made.

By strange coincidence, the two giants who I believe played the biggest roles in the development of jazz—Henderson and Duke Ellington—had a great deal in common.

Henderson, fondly known as Smack, was a chemistry major in his native Cuthbert, Georgia. He arrived in New York City scheduled to do postgraduate work at New York University. However, he soon found it took much more money for school in swift-paced

New York than he had anticipated back in the red-clay country of Georgia. Fortunately, he knew W. C. Handy and other popular songwriters of the day from back home and was soon playing piano background for record dates. What started out to be just a means toward finishing his education turned into a life's career.

Duke, on the other hand, went to New York from Washington, D.C., a fine-arts major with a scholarship to Pratt Institute of Art. He turned it down to continue his career as a musician.

Duke and Smack were pianists and possessed middle-class family backgrounds. Ellington's father was a white-collar government worker while Henderson's was a high school principal. The resemblance continued as both Henderson and Ellington became bandleaders, equally handsome, affable, and erudite. Henderson had preceded Ellington to New York by some years and was already a figure on the New York scene when Elmer Snowden, with young Ellington on piano, arrived in town.

New York at that period was piano crazy, perhaps because the combination of bootleg whiskey and relief from the tensions of the war provided a happy-go-lucky atmosphere for most people. Harlem was the stomping ground for many pianists—Luckey Roberts, Willie (The Lion) Smith, James P. Johnson, and the up-and-coming Fats Waller.

Thomas (Fats) Waller always stood a bit apart from the other greats of the instrument, because somehow he thought in terms of an orchestra. At a party or social gathering, he'd play the rags, stomps, or blues like everyone else. But that was only one side of him. Often, sitting in a cafe musing at the piano, he would explain to his enraptured audience as he struck a chord "this is the sax section," another chord "now, here comes the brass." He always strove to weave some sort of musical fabric into a tune.

It was not strange, therefore, that Fats became both Duke's and Smack's tutor at about the same time. Fats loved the big-band sound of our Roseland group, and he also enjoyed the imaginative smaller group that Duke led at the Kentucky Club. Fats sat in at Roseland, coaching Smack on orchestral speculations, and then went down to Duke's gig, where he also sat in.

Fletcher had a struggle with himself to start arranging—for one thing, he had Don Redman with his group who did arrangements and employed much of Fats' idiom in his writings. Meanwhile, Duke absorbed Fats' teachings and proceeded to utilize them until he brought his own inventive mind to jazz. This is where Duke and Fletcher started going in divergent directions. Smack fell asleep at the switch, while Duke, perhaps under the prodding of his manager, Irving Mills, explored every possible angle to make his music identifiable. This is one reason that Ellington chose to write his own compositions.

In the mid-twenties, however, Henderson's band was the talk of the town among musicians. His was the second Negro orchestra to play an all-season engagement at Roseland Ballroom on New York's Gay White Way. All the famous musicians hung around in front of the railing of our bandstand at Roseland, eager to hear (and borrow) from Smack. It seems like only yesterday when Frank Skinner, Archie Bleyer, Joe Glover, Georgie Bassman —to name only a few—would haunt Roseland in order to learn from the master.

Smack was not only the boss of his own bailiwick—New York —but of the entire country, for that matter. The main reason was our broadcasts from Roseland during the winter months we were in residence. Along with this, there were the eastern tours for booker Charlie Shribman, where we did tremendous repeat business, especially in the coalfields of Pennsylvania. As a matter of fact, we opened up the area for dance bands, and it was on one of those early tours that we met Pa and Ma Dorsey and their two lads, Tom and James.

Henderson's great popularity stemmed from the music, the many great musicians in the band, and the man himself. Smack was a man of imposing stature, about six feet two or so. His complexion was that of an octoroon, and in his youth he could have been mistaken for an Italian, as long as he was wearing his hat, because his hair was on the sandy side for his skin color. He was a pleasant man, gentle and thoughtful. He could be frivolous or serious, according to his mood. However, even in his zany moments, there would be overtones of gentility. His greatness also lay in his impeccable selection of sidemen—Louis Armstrong, Benny Carter, Coleman Hawkins, Don Redman.

Don played a most important role in the Henderson band. Short-statured, brown-skinned, this little giant arrived in New York in the mid-twenties from Piedmont, West Virginia. At the time he joined Fletcher, the band was a Dixielandish outfit, like most groups of the time. This loose approach did not satisfy Don, who, having been a music major in college, recognized the beauty that could be obtained if music were organized harmonically.

Redman set out to prove his point, over the objections of many musicians who felt that arranged music would take away from their creative ability. On the other hand, Don received a lot of encouragement from Smack, Will Vodery (who gave the jazz flavor to Flo Ziegfeld's shows), Will Marion Cook, and other leading Negro musicians.

The Henderson band assumed another dimension with Redman's arrangements. When Smack heard Louis Armstrong, in Chicago, playing licks that emphasized the dancing of a team called Dave and Tressie, this was quickly orchestrated the Redman way. The new concept (featuring figures made by the brass that paralleled the syncopation of the dancers) was copied immediately by other bands. Later, another of Don's ideas was paraphrased and parlayed into a career by Tommy Dorsey and others. Remember *Marie, Blue Skies,* and the parody of *On the Sunny Side of the Street* utilizing an obbligato countermelody with lyrics? Redman was the originator.

Actually, the Henderson band was a group of jazz giants—and about the biggest assortment of characters ever assembled to produce magnificent music. I was in my early twenties when Armstrong picked me as his replacement in Fletch's band. I joined reluctantly, and it took me a long time to overcome my awe at sitting in Louis' chair, playing the very same music and trying vainly to spark that band as Satchmo had. I almost had a nervous breakdown at first.

But Smack's easygoing attitude toward the men soon made me

feel at ease. His lack of aggessiveness in situations that called for
a strong hand, however, was sometimes resented by the fellows.
To illustrate: Bobby Stark (my section mate on trumpet) developed the habit of demanding money from Fletch at any time of
the day or night when he was in his cups. This often-repeated
scene was more than a little humorous as Bobby stood about five
feet one and didn't weigh 145 pounds soaking wet. Bobby would
charge Smack, head to chest, and in a belligerent manner snarl,
"Goddammit, Smack, give me some dough. It's drinking time, and
I'm thirsty." The guys would howl with laughter as little Bobby
bearded the larger man. Fletcher would smile tolerantly and
say, "No money for you, Bobby. You are drunk already, so head
for home."

Later, on a road trip, Bobby outdid himself. This was in Tulsa,
Oklahoma, and we were living at a hotel. Suddenly, we were
awakened by what sounded like somebody shooting into the side
of the hotel. Everybody jumped up and looked out the window.
There stood Bobby Stark hurling bricks at Fletcher's window,
punctuating each volley with a demand. It went like this:

"Smack, you SOB. I know you hear me."

Crash.

"Throw me twenty!"

Crash.

"Smack, you hear me? Throw me some dough. Make it ten!"

Crash.

By the time we reached Bobby, he was down to five dollars.

Bobby was a very quiet fellow until he got on the sauce, but
Smack was undoubtedly reincarnated from another age or planet.
He was just too gentle for his time. In my mind, he was the Ma-
hatma Gandhi of the jazz age.

Redman had a pretty easygoing attitude toward life too. One
time, he hit the Irish Sweepstakes for several thousand dollars.
The Henderson band was playing a concert at the Renaissance
Theater in Harlem, and the afternoon of the concert, Don bought
a brand new Cadillac with the money and proudly parked it
right in front of the theater. It seems to me that we had just

started playing when the band boy frantically signaled from the wings. A drunken taxi driver, he said, had demolished the new Cadillac. Don paused for a few seconds but then continued playing, seemingly unruffled. When the concert was over, he didn't even go out to look at the damage but remarked with a shrug, "Well, I guess that buggy just wasn't for me." The next day, he bought a new Buick.

As a band, we were car crazy. Since there were so few good cars in Harlem during that period, our departures on a road trip took on the aspect of a three-ring circus. Fletcher had a long black Packard roadster; Joe Smith, the trumpet player, had a chic, lean Wills St. Clair; drummer Kaiser Marshall sported a Buick. When these three beautiful cars were lined up in front of the Rhythm Club waiting for the rest of the guys, the pool players put down their cues, the poker games stopped, and all the other musicians gathered around to ooh and ah. I remember hearing Jelly Roll Morton, who seldom had a good word for anything, remark, "Damn, well, that's what I call a pretty sight."

Just about that time, Elmer Williams and Chu Berry, the tenor sax stars, rounded the corner of Seventh Avenue and 132nd Street on foot. Williams had his customary cigar in his mouth, but when he saw our classy caravan he almost swallowed the cigar, as he told Chu, "Now that's what I call the real big time. Those cats must be making *all* the money." We weren't really making *all* the money, but everybody in the band was very well paid.

We all welcomed these road trips, because we were paid even more money on the road, and then, too, there were lots of new little chicks in each town dedicated to helping us pass the time away. But for Fletcher and his wife, Leora, these trips were a lot of hard work. Our tours preceded the days of booking agents. Therefore, the Hendersons wrote many letters, sent loads of telegrams, and telephoned all over the eastern seaboard to coordinate the trips and consolidate the bookings.

Even with all the advance planning, sometimes there would be a goof, such as the time we jumped from Louisville to New York, only to be met by Mrs. Henderson saying, "Fletcher, what are you doing here? You're booked in Lexington tomorrow night." So we gassed up immediately, stopped by the bootlegger's and got some whiskey, and hit the road for Lexington, Kentucky. All of this in two and a half days, not over superhighways but bad roads. The guys in the band really earned the extra loot. We paid our dues.

Gradually, a few booking agents turned up on the scene. Along with Charlie Shribman, the next big operator was Ed Fishman, who started branching out from Harrisburg, Pennsylvania, and little by little more people entered the field. For groups that went on the road in later years with the aid and assistance of Music Corp. of America, Joe Glaser, and others, life was much simpler than for the Henderson band back in the twenties.

One experience I recall from our road tours is unforgettable. We had given up the caravan of cars and were riding a chartered bus. We got caught in an early spring freeze in the mountains of New Hampshire. The bus was unheated, and we had no overcoats; so we improvised by using newspapers. We'd place a newspaper between the undershirt and shirt, and another layer between the shirt and jacket. It kept us warm, but when the bus broke down climbing a mountain, we had to get out and push. Unaccustomed as we were to exercise, it was a real backbreaker pushing that bus up that mountain. To climax the situation, the top of the mountain was covered with ice, and hot as we had become pushing the bus up, we cooled off with fright as the bus slithered down the other side of the mountain. (Luckily, the bus was unharmed, and we were soon off and away again.)

During those road tours, we were notorious for not writing back home. Redman was one of the worst offenders. Days faded into weeks, and Don's wife began sending him telegrams, complaining because she had not heard from him. So Don bought a pretty box and some fancy wrapping paper, proceeded to gift wrap several sets of soiled underwear, and mailed the box home. The telegrams stopped arriving.

On our return to New York, there would always be a lot of record dates for us because of the snowballing of popularity on the

road. Along with the emergence of bookers for tours, the recording business picked up, since the tours produced new markets
for the music.

Curiously enough, although the Henderson band played a
variety of music on the tours, the record executives categorized
Smack's band as a stomp band. They didn't accept the fact that a
Negro band could play sweet, though, as a matter of fact, we
used to get tremendous applause at Roseland and other places for
playing waltzes beautifully. How unfortunate that we never recorded any of these waltz arrangements, and posterity can never
know the greatness of the Henderson band in that field.

Of course, the record business was very different in its early
days. I can't imagine a record executive today not being delighted
to capitalize on the music that was delighting the public. But in
the days of primitive recording, when each instrument would record into a separate horn and no bass drums were used, a lot of
the real flavor of the music could never be captured.

Smack was very disappointed at not being permitted to record
his famous *Rose* medley. This consisted of *Roses of Picardy* arranged by Charlie Dixon, *Broadway Rose* arranged by Benny
Carter, and several other popular songs of the day with the word
rose in the title, all in waltz tempo. Fletcher's disappointment was
not solely because his waltz medley had been vetoed, but also
because he had a predilection for rose. He wore rose-colored
shirts and ties and even bought a rose-colored Packard, or at least
ordered one. Unfortunately, Detroit didn't make cars in those
colors then. But then, they don't make musicians like Fletcher
Henderson today.

There is no question about Fletcher being the real big time for
his era, which spanned the years from 1923 until approximately
1944. At that time, he made his last significant effort when his
Jazz Train was presented in a Broadway night spot. This was an
attempt to depict and portray the evolutionary sequence of jazz.
It was a production complete with singers and dancers and
Fletcher's music.

Not only did Henderson achieve popularity and success from

his music, but he also was the catalyst for the birth of another star. Record producer and critic John Hammond influenced Smack to give his book of arrangements to an unknown but talented young clarinetist. In large measure because of Fletcher's book, Benny Goodman became an overnight sensation.

Goodman is not the only musician who owes a debt of gratitude to Fletcher Henderson. Jazz would not exist in its form today were it not for the many innovations, creativity, and contributions of Fletcher Henderson. He took the fundamentals of early jazz and molded them into a more permanent structure, from which our myriad contemporary forms of jazz have grown. Although many of our present-day jazz exponents may have forgotten, or never knew, what it was that Fletcher Henderson gave to jazz, there can be no doubt that this man shall be immortalized as one of the founding fathers of the only American art form.

Down Beat, June 3, 1965

The Business of Recording

A S FAR AS I can recall, my first awareness of the phonograph came in 1917. I remember winding the contraption with such vigor that it had to be repaired. In those days, the selection of records was small, and ours at home was perhaps typical, consisting mainly of marches, Caruso, some light classics (which I loathed), and some Bert Williams comedy monologues.

On arriving in New York City a few years later, I did not pay any attention to records, perhaps because there was quite a bit of talk among the older musicians against making records. They felt that they could protect their natural gifts better by not letting anyone copy their licks off a record. An extention of that attitude was the fact that certain saxophone and trumpet players covered their fingers with a handkerchief when they played, so that possible copiers wouldn't know how certain passages were made.

The combination of the elders' advice and my natural shyness kept me from the record scene, even after I was asked to record, because I never felt that I was good enough. One night, I was blowing pretty well in Goldgrabben's, a Harlem cabaret, when a fellow introduced himself, saying that he had a record date scheduled for the next week and that he would like to have me on the date. His name was Louis Hooper, and I remember telling him I would make it as he gave me his card. Actually, I didn't mean to accept, and immediately afterwards I was sorry I had. As the time drew near, I got more and more nervous. I knew that one was expected not to make any mistakes, and I also knew it was a rare thing for me to play an entire chorus without cutting a hog, as they called goofs in those days.

The day before the scheduled date, I phoned Hooper and told him to get somebody else, because I was not ready to record yet. Hooper just laughed and reassured me that it would be easy, just backing up a singer, and he was sure I could do it. So I let myself be talked into it.

When the great day arrived, I got up bright and early and started practicing on my horn (muted, of course). After about an hour, I got those buzzing chops that told me that I was as ready as I was going to get. Next, I was subway bound, after first stopping off at the bootlegger's to get some fortification. That was a good idea I found out after disembarking at Columbus Circle. I started looking for the address and hoped that the studio would not be in that tallest building across the street. But it was, and with quaking knees I took the elevator up, up, up (in those days, I was afraid of heights).

But once inside the studio, my fears vanished. Much to my delight and surprise, I found out that we were to accompany Rosa Henderson (no relation to Fletcher), who, with her husband Slim, was the cause of my leaving home with their ill-fated review *Go-Get-It.* In that show, I accompanied her vocals, so now I felt right at home.

I was fascinated by the ten or fifteen strangely shaped horns into which we were to blow. The horns resembled nothing I had ever seen before, made of wood, in various sizes, and all shaped like a violet. Shortly, we settled down to business, and I made my first record, way back in 1922.

During the next few years, I made several recordings with Monette Moore, Virginia Liston, and another one with Rosa Henderson. Then came the big time—recording with Fletcher Henderson, whom I joined in 1926. I shall never forget the thrill of playing solo on *Stampede* and *The Jackass Blues.* It was hard work, requiring considerable concentration. However, there were humorous moments on some sessions.

One such moment concerned Coleman Hawkins, that celebrated creator of tenor saxophone style. With his customary reticence, Bean—as we guys in the band nicknamed him—had never mentioned his adulation for Adrian Rollini, who was the best performer of all time on the bass saxophone. We had, of course, noticed his interest in Rollini's hot bass sax licks whenever they'd meet at a session (which was quite often back in those days). But we never guessed the full extent of his admiration. So, we thought he was just kidding when he told trombonist Jimmy Harrison that he had enough money to pay cash for anything he wanted, including a bass sax. But he wasn't joking.

When he first turned up with a new bass saxophone, flourishing a receipt stamped "paid in full," Jimmy teased him by asking, "Who is going to play that thing? Bean, you must be crazy!"

Hawk answered, "What do you mean who's going to play it? I'm going to play it, of course." That led right into their customary caustic kidding, each claiming to be the better musician.

We were to record the next day. Hawk beat everybody to the studio and was busy tuning up the monster when we arrived. The irrepressible Jimmy delayed the start of the session by exclaiming to Fletcher, "My God, Smack, you didn't tell me that Adrian was gonna make this date!"

Hawk, for once, refused the challenge and even pretended not to hear. We took our places and did not have to wait long for the unveiling of the new sound as Bean, featured as usual, started whomping away at his chorus right after the introduction.

Then pandemonium broke loose, triggered by Harrison's hee-haws of derision. Jimmy laughed until he had tears in his eyes, but Coleman kept on playing, growing more agitated as he cajoled, coaxed, and did everything he could think of to make the beast sound musical. Finally, Fletcher broke down, too, and started laughing along with us, as he waved the rhythm section to a halt. Bean gave up. He packed up and stalked out of the session, muttering to himself something about the damn mouthpiece was no good. Exit Coleman Hawkins, dragging his nemesis with him. Later, I heard that he returned the bass sax that same day. And that was one of the few Henderson records without a Hawk solo.

Another session worthy of comment is the one that made a record producer the laughingstock of Broadway. First, however, I should say that in those days most people felt that a musician played with more native abandon when he was full of alcohol. This producer believed this implicitly, so whenever he headed a date, there would always be plenty of whiskey or gin. Back in those prohibition days, since all schnapps came from the same bathtub, the only difference would be the flavor. Gin, perhaps, was the most disastrous of the lot, for bootleggers laced the concoction of juniper essence and alcohol with a touch of ether.

When this particular record date was called, New York was in the grip of a heat wave, and the tiny studio felt like the lower regions of Dante's *Inferno.* As we cut the first two sides, sweat dripped from everybody in buckets. By that time, the gin had us feeling no pain, but when we took a break, somebody came up with the bright idea of continuing with iced gin. That was the beginning of the end, because the producer took a milk bottle full of iced gin to the sound engineer, whereupon the two of them proceeded to reminisce about earlier records they had made together.

As they talked on and on, the musicians began to feel the effects of the hot room and the cold gin. One by one they draped themselves on chairs or wherever they could find a spot to stretch out and go to sleep. The next thing we knew, it was daylight. As the fellows started to wake up, the producer was seen holding up the engineer by his snores alone. It seems that somebody had been a bit heavy with the ether in that batch of gin. Anyway, after coffee, we staggered through the other two sides and limped home to finish sleeping off our recording session.

For a musician, the quickest entry into public acceptance as a composer is via the phonograph record. One of my unfulfilled ambitions was to join the ranks of those who made it. Although I have written a few tunes that turned out to be good vehicles, they were popularized by others, a turn of events that can be blamed on my stupidity and others' cupidity.

About thirty-five years ago I had the band in the Empire Ballroom, across the street from the Roseland on Broadway. We began broadcasting. Neldon Hurd (who played trombone in the band), Edgar Sampson (saxophone and arranger), and I cooked up a theme for the broadcasts. My contribution was the bridge; Neldon produced the theme, and Edgar came up with the obbligato and arrangement. We played it in a ballad tempo, slow but with a beat. I had a chance to record the tune, among others, for Irving Mills, but I refused to accept the date because he wanted a smaller group than the twelve pieces that comprised my band at the Empire.

After seventeen months at the ballroom, we went on tour, hoping that the fan mail resulting from the broadcasts indicated that we had built a name. But we didn't draw flies, and to make matters worse, our library mysteriously disappeared in a taxi in Washington, D.C. When, again, there was only a small crowd at the dance that night, I lost heart, gave up the struggle, and joined Luis Russell's band.

Two years later, in 1934, I joined Duke Ellington. Turning on the radio one night, I was amazed to hear Benny Goodman stomping out our old theme, now called *Stompin' at the Savoy*. The next day in a music store, I learned that composers' credits were noted as Goodman, Chick Webb, and Sampson! And they still are. That tune could have meant so much to my catalog of more than fifty unplayed songs. I really goofed in not making that record date.*

Then there was the episode of the four deuces vs. the three aces. This happened in mid-Atlantic during one of the inevitable poker sessions in the Ellington organization. My luck was running as good as the seas were running high. One by one, the game had

*In a letter to the editor, subsequently published in *Down Beat*, Edgar Sampson commented:

". . . When I joined Stewart's orchestra, he needed a theme song, and I brought in a chorus of one of my compositions, which he accepted. We called it *Misty Morn* because we went on the air at midnight.

"At the end of the summer I returned to Chick Webb's orchestra at the Savoy. It was there that I made a complete arrangement of *Stompin' at the Savoy*. Benny Goodman and Webb made recordings of the tune and became associated with it.

"In the many years that I have been composing, I can truthfully say that I have never accepted credit for material that I didn't write. It seems strange that after 30 years, Stewart and Hurd would have illusions that they composed *Stompin' at the Savoy*." [Ed.]

dwindled until only two players were left, just Duke and Fat Stuff (that's what he used to call me).

The first face-up card that he dealt me was an ace, and I didn't dare look at it hard because I had already peeped at my hole card, another ace. His up card was a deuce, so in order not to frighten him out before there was something in the pot, I bet in a very mild fashion. My next card was insignificant, but I bet a little stronger, despite his hitting himself with another deuce. The battle was really on when a second ace leaped off the deck and I had two aces showing against his two deuces.

I thought it best at this point to indicate my overwhelming supremacy by betting a sizable sum, and I fully expected Duke to say take it, but he didn't concede—he raised me! I might add at this point that Ellington's idea of strategy was to hang on until the last card and then attempt to overpower his opponent with a huge bet, unless his opponent's overlay was in sight. So, as I figured out his hand, he had to have either two pairs or three deuces, and if he had deuces back to back, it would have been unlikely for him not to have demonstrated his strength by betting stronger. I deduced, therefore, that he had two pairs so the chances of his catching up with my three aces was remote.

Bet and raise, bet and raise until all the money on the table was in the pot. Then, he bet me fifty dollars more; being out of cash, I put the rights to one of my tunes in the pot. The last card was dealt, and Duke dealt himself another deuce. The boat seemed to stand still as I realized that I had lost the pot and my tune, *Morning Glory.*

The question "what was it like recording with Ellington?" is frequently asked me. My answer has always been that it is a unique experience, unlike anything I've ever encountered before or since. On reflection, it just doesn't seem possible that it has been twenty years since I recorded with Duke!

At this juncture, I no longer remember my first or last recording date with the organization, but I do recall with vivid detail the unorthodox manner in which Duke operates. His modus operandi has to be seen to be believed.

Sometimes at the recording studio, many pages of manuscript

would be passed out, and we would proceed to run down the arrangements once or twice. Then, after a bit of reflection, Duke would tell us to get out the pencils. This meant there were going to be changes, and he would proceed with instructions such as, "We'll start this at Bar two of the original intro, then continue as is on down to Bar sixteen of Letter F, segue back to the fourth bar of the intro and, this time, let the brass calm down while the saxes shout out that 'good-old-timey' feeling." Sometimes the final results bore little relation to the original arrangement.

Other times, we'd get all set up, and Duke would say, "C'm here, Barney. Remember what you played that night in Oshkosh? Oh, you remember, it was raining and that gal in the red dress got so excited she started dancing on the bandstand and the cops had to take her off."

If Barney Bigard or Johnny Hodges or whoever didn't recall the incident or the lick, Dumpy, as we called Duke, would play it on the piano, saying, "It went like this." After that had been straightened out, Duke might say, "I like that! Hey, Cootie, how about growling behind this? Then, we'll have the sax section creep in on a D-flat major chord. Harry, you tonic the chord at the top of your baritone. Saxes, hit the chord and hold it until Barney does the waterfall, then Brown will take over the melody."

The tune most times would evolve from a lick or a chordal sequence. Such is the genius of Ellington that these impromptu and imaginative methods resulted in pure gems.

An approximation of an Ellington type of session occurred in France in 1939. Hugues Panassie had proposed that I record for him the next time I was in Europe. That was when we had dinner in New York. I arrived in France with Ellington some months later. Panassie called me early one morning and said, "Let's make the date." I protested that I was unprepared, having nothing down on paper, though I had the tunes thought out in my head. However, Panassie explained that Django Reinhardt, the great gypsy guitarist, was going to record with us and could hear and play anything. I was dubious but consented.

We arrived at the studio (Barney Bigard, bassist Billy Taylor, and I) and were crushed to see how old and beat up the building was. We found Panassie and Django already there in the dilapidated studio. We looked at each other and couldn't figure how in the world anybody could record in a setup like this. But it was too late to back out, so we unpacked our horns, while wondering where the drummer was.

Deciding not to waste time, I began to blow a simple blues for Django to learn. Django spoke little English, if any, but there was no strain of communication between us. But never having heard him before, I was unaware of his virtuosity and quick ear. To my astonishment, he proceeded not only to play the blues but to embellish them with an evocative gypsy quality. But still no drummer. Panassie felt things were good the way they were and said, "That sounded great! Let's make it." On this happy note, I decided to expose Django to a more complex tune of mine, *Finesse*. (In later years, this was renamed *Night Wind* and my buddy, Billy Taylor, was given composer credit.)

The rest of the tunes that I had composed for the date were recorded in quick succession. Once down for rehearsal, then on wax. And the drummer never showed. But all in all, it was a memorable experience, and I'll always be grateful to Panassie for giving me my first opportunity to record with the great Django. In later years, I recorded with him several more times, but the initial exposure was the greatest.

One of the most intriguing facets of the recording business is the element of chance. Actually, it is like a crap game loaded with a larger amount of misses than hits. Many a proven artist, with a string of hits behind him, can sometimes be humpty-dumped off the popularity throne overnight by a neophyte. Conversely, a newcomer can rise from coffee and cakes to champagne and filet mignon in less time than it takes to write about his success. Nobody can guarantee what will happen in the record business.

This pertains particularly to the unexpected sounds that sometimes creep unwonted onto tape. Lionel Hampton's grunting, Erroll Garner's foot stomping, and Duke Ellington's eerie humming are well known, and every engineer who records these peo-

ple is aware of their idiosyncrasies, takes them into account, and
exercises caution by placing the microphones where they are
least likely to pick up these extraneous sounds.

But over and above the known, there is always the unknown
and unforeseen that can bollix up recordings. Among these are the
vagaries of human personality. There may be the star whose mood
is ever-changing, who one time wants to be one of the boys, working in the midst of his fellows, and another time will demand complete isolation in a booth. There can be the sweetie pie from
whom you never know what to expect. When her fancy strikes,
she'll waste time and studio money regaling her captive audience
with dirty stories. At another time, she will swoop in, surrounded
by her not inconsiderable entourage, and be all business, and
woe betide any character who doesn't get the message.

The sound technicians and engineers have to be on their toes.
It may be my imagination, but it seems that a lot of the time
there's considerable one-upmanship played by the technicians
and the leaders. I've seen them almost come to blows over how a
certain sound should be reproduced. Many a time a leader has
been infuriated when the guy in the control booth has arbitrarily
balanced a group contrary to the leader's wishes. Somehow, they
don't seem to hear sound in the same way. In more recent years,
the split has become even worse, as producers, leaders, and technicians battle it out, and in these cases, it's a toss-up as to whose
projection will emerge on the recording.

Back in the Henderson days, we had a strange situation in spite
of a leader and producer who saw eye to eye. Leonard Joy, who
really knew what recording was all about, was the producer, and
he was in complete agreement with Smack's featuring Russell
Smith, our first trumpet man. Russ played very beautifully in
the upper register, and that day his chops were in fine shape.
Everything started off perfectly—we were ready and on time for
once, and we made what sounded to us in the studio like a master, a perfect performance, on the first take. But on hearing the
playback, sixteen bars from the end, right in the middle of Smith's
solo—as he soared like an angel and the saxophones intoned a

lovely accord—we heard a foreign tweetering sound. Brows furrowed, frowns replaced smiles of satisfaction, and everybody looked around with a what-happened expression on his face. Fletcher jumped up from the piano to head for the control booth and was met by Joy, whose ever-present pipe was wigwagging signals of concern.

Joy, however, asked mildly, "What was the noise? Did someone move his chair around? Was it the drummer's foot pedal? Oh, well, let's make it again and try to be more quiet. That was a beautiful take, and I doubt that we'll get another as good."

But he was wrong. We proceeded to blow another beautiful take, almost holding our breath when we were not blowing. Then, when we listened to that playback, the distortion was present again, at the identical place. Fletcher, for once, lost his famed composure and said to Joy, "This noise has to be in the equipment because I know damn well that it wasn't out here." Leonard replied, "Okay, take time out while I have the engineer check."

This was done, and we returned to our places, kind of bored, since the edge had worn off, but we were still baffled about the weird sound continuing to crop up. It did again on the third take, and subsequently the tune was dropped, and we went on to something else. We never did find out where the unwelcome sound came from or why. My pet theory, which I've never dared mention before, is that there was a mouse in the studio that wanted to get into the act.

In the early days, such a thing was not impossible. The studios were quite primitive compared with today's. Air conditioning was unknown. Separate horns (instead of mikes) for each instrument to blow into limited the drummer, for instance, to temple blocks, cymbals, and a few other effects. Snare drums and bass drums could not be recorded. The takes were recorded on acetate so if a flub was made, the entire effort had to be scrapped. Not so since the advent of tape, which makes it possible to snip from a great beginning, add it to the best middle, splicing perhaps a solo from another take, and finish off with the best ending from several, and wind up with a virtuoso performance.

This reminds me of a recent Duke Ellington session I attended as a spectator. The band was recording the music originally played at Grace Cathedral, in San Francisco. On a previous day, the band had recorded the bulk of the material from this concert and was now doing some tie-ins. Duke called out, "Get out ITBG [*In the Beginning God*]. We're only going to do bars 272, 273, and 274." The fellows leafed through their sheafs of music to find the part.

Johnny Hodges looked in vain and finally called out, "Hey, Duke, I don't have any music! Give me the notes."

Duke answered urbanely, "It's only three notes. Just play the blues, man. Play the blues."

This brought great laughter from the fellows, and Duke never did give him any further clues. I presume he just played the blues, as instructed, and I am looking forward to this album's release so I can hear how Hodges' part fits.

Splicing tape is not the only innovation that has helped recording. Sidney Bechet perhaps inspired a great variety of potentiality in sound when he made his famous one-man band recording, playing piano, drums, bass, clarinet, and soprano saxophone. Later, Les Paul and Mary Ford parlayed a guitar and the human voice, by virtue of multiple recording, into a huge success. The echo chamber, too, has played its part in building a small voice into a big one.

Yes, the recording industry and techniques have come a long way since those early days of hand-wound phonographs and the dog who gazed adoringly into the big horn that reproduced the sound of his master's voice.

Down Beat, April 7, 1966

Boy Meets King
(Louis Armstrong)

S ATCHMO'S TIME AND PLACE in the history of music is firmly etched, chronicled, and, thanks to the phonograph recordings, entirely documented. Future students and researchers will certainly benefit from this fortunate circumstance. Consider how much of the other early jazzmen's influences have been lost, because of the sublime unawareness of the sociological impact of this music and its early creators. But happily, Joe Oliver recorded the first true ragtime ensembles for Gennett—at least, he was the first one I ever heard.

In those early days of jazz, the real shape and substance of what was to be in music came from people such as Ford Dabney and William Grant Still in New York (they wrote the first ragtime arrangements back in 1910), from Doc Cook in Chicago, and from Joe (King) Oliver. These men, plus Dave Peyton and Erskine Tate in Chicago, helped comprise an atmosphere and proving ground for Louis Armstrong. There in Chicago, away from the catch-as-catch-can climate of New Orleans, putting himself past the rough-and-ready musical chaos of the river, Louis came to maturity. He added his magic to the pastel of progress in music with his horn when he left New Orleans in 1922 to join Oliver's Creole Jazz Band.

During the period when Joe Oliver was around New York, which was after his Chicago days, I got to know him through his nephew, Dave Nelson. Joe's best playing days were over, but he recounted many tales of how he and "Dipper" (Louis) upset everybody when they played together. But Papa Joe's days of glory were fading while Louis' star was ascending.

Every record Louis made was a winner. On his personal appearances, he'd cream the crowd by hitting 100 high C's as the band counted them one by one. Then, the new King would top this effort with a high F. Often King Oliver would be in the audience, rooting for his pupil, along with everybody else. There was no jealousy despite the ironic turn of events. Fate had denied Oliver's sharing in the great acclaim.

I remember Joe's telling me how sorry he was that New York did not hear them together. I asked him why they had preferred Chicago, and he told me there had been two good reasons, both of them spelled "syndicate." No booker wanted to incur the ill will of the Chicago syndicate that operated the club (Lincoln Gardens) where they played. Even if a booker dared attempt a New York deal, there was no place in New York where they could play. Later, Louis got so good that more and more offers came his way. Joe reluctantly bade Satchmo Godspeed, and the greatest team the world of jazz was ever to know was no longer.

When Satchmo left Chicago in 1924 to join Fletcher Henderson's band in New York, there was quite a bit of old New Orleans still clinging to him. His was not the fictional, courtly, genteel New Orleans of moonlit nights tinged with romance and honeysuckle. What he carried with him was the aroma of red beans and rice, with more than a hint of voodoo and "gris-gris." He conveyed this to the world by the insouciant challenge of his loping walk, the cap on his head tilted at an angle, which back home meant: "Look out! I'm a bad cat—don't mess with me!" These, plus the box-back coat and the high-top shoes, all added to young Louis' facade in those days.

However, when Louis returned to his Chicago south-side stomping grounds in 1925, the youngster had changed into a worldly man, a sophisticated creator of music that people looked up to. He had arrived, and a world was waiting for the king of the trumpet. The climate for his homecoming couldn't have been better, owing to the south-side theaters' emulating Paul Ash's successful band shows in the Loop.

Louis started drawing huge crowds that came just to be sent by his horn, whether he was playing with the theater bands of Dave Peyton or Erskine Tate, both of whom vied for his talent. They competed so vigorously that sometimes he would appear with both of them on the same night. The movie or the stage show took second place to Satch's specialty act in the overture.

Louis was quite an eater in those days, and for many years he carried a lot of weight, but he burned up a lot of that food in his musical exertions. Louis really had, and still has, great physical stamina, doubtless because of his love of sports during his formative years. Buster Bailey, the elegant delineator of the clarinet, used to tell about the fun around Chicago in the early twenties. Summers were spent at the beach with Darnell Howard, Guy Kelly, Johnny Dodds, and others cavorting like porpoises in Lake Michigan. Louis outswam almost everybody, doing at least a mile a day. This sort of training paid off later, as endurance and breath control enhanced his imaginative talents in scaling the ultimate heights of his instrument.

Our mutual friend, Luis Russell, told this one on Satchmo, which happened during those Chicago days. He and Louis were invited to dinner, and the hostess went all out preparing a sumptuous banquet for her distinguished guests. Russell said they sat down to a huge table loaded with roast beef, fried chicken, mixed greens, mashed potatoes, red beans, and corn on the cob—this feast was topped off with peach cobbler and ice cream. The guys paid proper tribute and ate and ate, while the hostess glanced from one to the other in pride at their appreciation. Finally, there was nothing left but the chicken bones. The woman said, "My, it sure is nice to have somebody enjoy my cooking like you boys did." Then Louis said, "I know what you mean, but if you *only* had some rice to go with those red beans, I could start all over again!"

Although it has been forty years since I first met Ol' Dipper, as he was nicknamed then, I don't feel that I really know Daniel L. Armstrong. Somehow, I suspect that most of his disciples are no closer than I am to knowing this solid cornerstone of American jazz who is largely responsible for the shape and structure of this art form. Nevertheless, Louis remains an enigma even to his close friends, presenting an ever-changing kaleidoscope-montage of moods.

Sometimes he is gregarious, extroverted, loyal, and considerate. He is the sort of person who buys a youngster a trumpet, or pays the rent for some unfortunate. These things he never speaks of. Then again, he sometimes behaves as if there were some compulsion to prove he is the same as the rest of us, excepting for his great talent. Then there are the times that he presents a withdrawn, glum attitude like a smoldering volcano primed to erupt at any moment; however, this phase is always temporary, and the sunshine inevitably beams in Satch's smile.

Before his audiences, he is always the lovable, mugging, blowing-up-a-storm Louis the Great. His feet may be killing him or that famed Swiss Kriss acting up, but all that he shows to his public is a handkerchief-waving, eye-popping *Hello, Dolly* type of communication—to the delight of most. Many a time I have sat in an audience, transfixed by the imagination, stamina, and, above all, the innate sense of timing Louis possesses in such superlative abundance. He can take one note and swing you into bad health on that same note. His rhythmic concept is *that* profound.

Despite these obvious attributes, there are those who do not understand or appreciate the master. These, of course, are far outnumbered by the legions who feel that Satch may well be the present-day personification of Moses whom they would gladly follow to the promised land of jazz.

How regrettable it is that, despite the current recognition and acclaim, simultaneously his name and great efforts are anathema to many. Some of the musicians who have succumbed to the siren song of contemporary commercialism project the belief that anything old is of no value. Others consciously resent Louis' antebellum Uncle Tomism. The youngsters object to his ever-present grin, which they interpret as Tomming. This I feel is a misunderstanding. No matter where Louis had been brought up, his natural ebullience and warmth would have emerged just as creative and strong. This is not to say that even today, in an unguarded moment, a trace of the old environment, a fleeting lapse into the jargon of his youth will make some people cringe with embarrassment.

There is justification for both sides of opinion on Louis today. I would not presume to pass judgment. However, I will say that I do feel grateful to have existed in the same musical environment as the King.

This exposure started at the old Savoy Ballroom in New York City. I was playing with a now long-forgotten band, Leon Abby's Savoy Bluesicians. Louis was then with Henderson's outfit, and it was making one of its rare Harlem appearances.

Our trumpet section consisted of Demas Dean on first trumpet, myself, and another man whose name I've forgotten. We decided that the only proper way to enjoy Armstrong was to help the mood along with liquid refreshments. So we all filled Coca-Cola bottles with our favorite beverage. I chose gin, which was a mistake, because the combination of Louis' artistry and that gin caused me to be put out of the ballroom in the middle of the dance. This was a most humiliating climax to an eventful evening. For some reason, I was bounced out of the joint merely for showing my appreciation of Louis' high notes! Every time he'd end on a soaring F, I tossed a Coke bottle, and you couldn't even hear the crash over the applause. But the bouncers didn't understand.

While most of the musicians drank a good deal, Armstrong never was a fellow for hanging out in the bars much. In New York, on any given night, you could run into almost anybody who considered himself a real blower in Big John's or the Mimo Club when Bojangles ran it. But not Louis.

So I was pleasantly surprised one night when I fell into the Brittwood Bar, which was near the Savoy Ballroom, and I saw Satch sitting there. By this time, we knew each other on sight. I called him Pops and he called me Boy. He still calls me Boy, and I don't remember his ever calling me by name. But that night at the Brittwood, I had had enough whiskey to make me sleepy. I went to a rear table, sat down, and promptly fell asleep. The next thing I knew, I heard a gravel voice saying, "Boy, get up and get you some Pluto water. Yeah, Pluto water, that's what you need. You should be 'shamed of yourself, young as you are drinking all of that whiskey. I'm gonna tell you something. If you don't quit acting the fool with that juice, they gonna be giving you flowers, and you won't even smell 'em." Then Louis laughed and left. There was a hint of a sequel, though, because for the next few years, whenever our paths crossed, he'd say "hi, Pluto" as he passed.

From the time Louis catapulted onto the New York scene, everybody and his brother tried to play like him, with the possible exception of Johnny Dunn and Bubber Miley. Now, with the passing years, Satch's impact has diminished to the point where no one consciously tries to sound like him, but at the same time, almost every player in the throes of improvisation plays something that can be traced to Louis Armstrong.

Louis was the musician's musician. I was only one of his ardent admirers. I tried to walk like him, talk like him. I bought shoes and a suit like the Great One wore. I remember a time that a few of us—Ward Pinkett, Gus Akins, and a couple of others—thought it would be a good idea to stand under Louis' window and serenade him. This occurred to us in the wee hours after we had emerged from a bar. We had just got started when the cop on the beat discouraged us by saying, "Get the hell off the streets before I run ya in."

There were so many fellows showering Satchmo with unblushing adulation that I didn't think he knew me from the rest of the young trumpet players. One night, when I was playing with Elmer Snowden at the Nest Club, I was startled to spot Louis, Buster Bailey, and Big Green in the crowd. (Bailey and trombonist Green also were in Henderson's band.) Snowden had spotted them first and called a tune on which I was supposed to solo as long as I wanted to, set my own tempo, and show off. I must have played pretty well, because Louis and other fellows in Henderson's band took to dropping in from time to time. Since I was partly responsible for their attendance, I was really set up.

But the really big moment of my life came a month or so later. One evening at the Nest Club, an attendant came to the stand and said there was a phone call for me. I wondered who could be calling me on the job. I couldn't believe it when a voice said, "I've got a job for you, Boy." I thought I recognized the gravel voice but wasn't sure if maybe it wasn't a gag, so I played along. I think I answered, "Yeah? Where is this job?" The guy laughed and said, "This is Louis, and I want you to take my place with Smack. I'm going back to Chicago." It really was Louis, and the offer was for real! I took the job with Fletcher, but my heart wasn't in it. The horn wasn't born that could follow the King—and I still feel that way.

A few years after the Coke-bottle episode, Louis played the Savoy again. I wanted to hear him but had been barred from the premises because of my misbehavior. So I pulled my coat collar up to cover my face, bought a ticket, and slunk past Big George the doorman, determined to conduct myself like a gentleman this time.

Besides Louis with one band, Benny Carter was also leading a group, his first big band. I stood off to the side of the stand, trying not to be noticed by the floorwalker. All went well, and I was thoroughly enjoying Louis. Unfortunately, when his set ended, Benny spied me and beckoned me to come up on the stand. I shook my head no, meaning: "No, I'm not here." Benny would not take no for an answer, however, and before I knew it, I was on the stand playing *Tiger Rag*. To this day, I don't know why, but I received a very good hand from the crowd. Instead of being elated, I tried to get off the stand and become part of the woodwork again, but Benny struck up *Tiger Rag* again, and this time the crowd gave me a big hand. I wasn't put out, but I couldn't enjoy the rest of the evening; I expected every moment to be given the bum's rush.

A few days later, I ran into Louis on the street and went over to say hello, but he only grunted and walked away. We weren't tight like that anymore for several years, and I found out subsequently from Zutty Singleton that Louis thought that I had tried to cut him! Honestly, Louis, I have never tried to. As far as I am concerned, you are the Boss and always will be.

Jabbo Smith obviously didn't share my feelings, and as a matter of fact, Jabbo tried on several occasions to prove he was better on trumpet than King Louis. He was never able to convince any of the other musicians, but he certainly tried hard.

One such occasion comes to mind. It was an Easter Monday morning breakfast dance at Rockland Palace, Harlem's biggest dancehall. Jabbo was starring in Charlie Johnson's band from Small's Paradise, but Don Redman's band, featuring Satch, from Connie's Inn was the top attraction. It was a beautiful sight—no flower garden could compete with the beauty of the gals' bonnets. There was also intense factionalism in the air, because no one from Charleston, S.C., would concede Armstrong's superiority over their hometown boy, Jabbo. We musicians tried to tell the Charlestonians that while Jabbo was great, Louis was King. We needn't have bothered. For weeks before the dance, arguments raged, bets were made, and, finally, the great moment came.

I rushed up from Roseland, as soon as the last note was played, intending to get a front-row view of the battle. But when I entered the hall, I found that more than a hundred musicians had beaten me to any choice spot, so I pulled out my horn and got on the stand with Charlie's band. Nobody said anything, which figured, because I always sat in with anybody around town in those days.

Jabbo was standing out in front, and I'll say this, he was *blowing*—really coming on like the angel Gabriel himself. Every time he'd fan that brass derby on a high F or G, Altis, his buddy from Small's, would yell, "Play it, Jabbo! Go ahead, Rice!" (Everybody from Charleston called each other Rice. It was the hometown nickname.) "Who needs Louis?" he yelled, "You can blow him down anytime." Although there were only about a hundred or so of the South Carolina contingent in the crowd of some 2,000, these people created a real uproar for their idol. When Johnson's set ended with Jabbo soaring above the rhythm and the crowd noise, everybody gave them a big hand. I could tell from the broad grin on Jabbo's face that he felt that once and for all he'd shown Satch who was king.

Then, all of a sudden, the shouts and applause died down as Louis bounced onto the opposite stage, immaculate in a white suit. Somehow, the way the lights reflected off his trumpet made the instrument look like anything but a horn. It looked as if he were holding a wand of rainbows or a cluster of sunlight, something from out of this world. I found out later that I was not the only one who had the strong impression of something verging on the mystical in Louis' entrance. I can still see the scene in my mind's eye. I've forgotten the tune, but I'll never forget his first note. He blew a searing, soaring, altissimo, fantastic high note and held it long enough for every one of us musicians to gasp. Benny Carter, who has perfect pitch, said, "Damn! That's high F!" Just about that time, Louis went into a series of cadenzas and continued into his first number.

Since everyone is not a trumpet player and cannot know how the range of the instrument has grown over the years, I should explain how significant a high F was. Back in the twenties, the acceptable high-note range for the trumpet was high C and to hit or play over C made the player exceptional. That is until Louis came along with his strong chops, ending choruses on F. We guys strained might and main to emulate him but missed most of the time. That is why we were so flabbergasted at Satchmo's first note. Lots of guys ruined their lips and their career trying to play like Satchmo.

Louis never let up that night, and it seemed that each climax topped its predecessor. Every time he'd take a break, the applause was thunderous, and swarms of women kept rushing the stand for his autograph. They handed him everything from programs to whiskey bottles to put his signature on. One woman even took off her pants and pleaded with him to sign them!

Years ago, Erskine Tate told me this story about the time Louis was doing a satire on something called *The Preaching Blues*. He was wearing a frock coat and battered top hat, singing a kind of ring-chant tune with Louis making calls like a Baptist preacher, while the audience made the responses. Eventually one sister became confused as the mood grew more and more frantic, and her voice could be heard above the crowd. She was easily spotted because when the number ended, she rushed down the aisle shouting, "Don't stop, Brother Louis, don't stop." The audience in the theater broke up.

Louis has retained over the years his direct, uncluttered approach to his music, preferring to surround himself with competent people rather than easing the burden by choosing dynamic personalities or instrumentalists who would be able to give him the relief he has earned. The King still carries the ball.

This, of course, is a recent development, as the original Louis Armstrong All-Stars were just what the name implied. That was the group that at one time boasted Jack Teagarden, Barney Bigard, Earl Hines, Big Sid Catlett, and a phenomenal young star on bass, Arvell Shaw. It turned out to be a wise move on the part of whoever made the decision when Satch shed the overwhelmingly ponderous big band of the thirties and early forties and returned in 1947 to the Hot Five concept with which he began. He regained the winning element of spontaneous freewheeling, a proper framework for his talents. Armstrong's big-band efforts were, as a whole, constricting him, reminding some observers of a champion race horse pulling a heavy junk wagon. This was the effect, whether the background was a fully manned Hollywood type of creation or the more sympathetic Harlem-trained big-band crew that had the verve and also the right feeling but, unfortunately, usually played quite out of tune.

The question crops up invariably: why does Satch drive himself so hard on those interminable one-nighters? He still maintains a schedule that would wreck the health of a weaker musician, but lately there have been indications that the passing years are mellowing Armstrong. For example, I was surprised to read a recent statement credited to him in which he publicly came out strongly for civil rights.

My thoughts immediately went back to the period when a bunch of us, including Roy Eldridge, Erskine Hawkins, Cootie Williams, Dizzy Gillespie, and myself, tried to form what we tentatively labeled Trumpet Council of America. The purpose was to help gifted youngsters whom we would meet during our tours, recommending them to bandleaders, giving them encouragement, and also buying them instruments if necessary. This idea germinated in Los Angeles, where we had one meeting, but we planned to organize in New York. We felt that we needed Armstrong's name to assure success. We wanted him to be at least our honorary president. I was nominated to get in touch with Louis about it.

When I went backstage at the Apollo to sound him out, Pops was in good humor, asking about mutual chums, but when I brought up the idea about the association, his good spirits faded. He said gruffly, "You'll have to see Joe about that." As I vainly tried to explain that Joe Glaser, his manager, would not be interested and that all we wanted was the use of his name, his reply never changed. He still said, "See Joe."

There's no doubt that Glaser has exercised a tremendous influence on Louis, and perhaps this is fitting and proper. However, it is refreshing to note that at long last Louis has arrived at a point when he occasionally speaks his own piece.

Louis has bestowed so many gifts upon the world that it is almost impossible to assess in which area his definitive impact has been most felt. My vote would be for his tremendous talent of communication. As profoundly creative as his trumpet ability is, I would place this in a secondary position. He was revered mostly by other professionals, whereas his gravel-voiced singing has carried the message far and wide, to regions and places where not only was the music little known and the language foreign, but where there also was the further barrier of a political system having labeled jazz as decadent. But when Satchmo sang, the entire picture changed. People saw the truth.

Another, perhaps curious, phenomenon is the reaction of some Americans abroad who, back home, never cared about jazz, Louis, or the Negro people. But when you meet them overseas, they say with pride, "That's *our* Satchmo." Sometimes, this inadvertent awakening leads to a permanent change of attitude—at least, the thinking Negro musician likes to believe so.

To some people, Louis projects the "ambassador" by acclamation, the creator by virtue of his God-given gifts. To me, it remains more than ample just to have existed in the same musical atmosphere as the King. The great debt I owe him for setting the stage, worldwide, for American jazz music, I can never repay. The New Orleans waif who in some ways never left home, who gave music more than he'll ever take from it, deserves further recognition from the American people.

Baseball has its Hall of Fame, other nations have places where statues of the noteworthy are exhibited, and I propose that we erect a suitable monument to Ambassador Louis. We really should pay homage to one of the immortals of this original American art form.

Down Beat, July 15, 1965

The Father of Swing Trombone
(Jimmy Harrison)

"MANY ARE CALLED but few are chosen" is an adage that in this instance projects my thoughts perfectly. The instance at hand is James Henry Harrison, who made tremendous contributions to jazz with his trombone, and despite the thirty-six years since his death, he lives on.

Musicians who were not even born when Jimmy was in his heyday continue the line by playing what he created. From time to time, I hear something either in someone's playing or perhaps a jazz lick in an arrangement that Jim created long ago. But if I were to mention the name of Jimmy Harrison in a group of musicians or jazz fans, most wouldn't know who I was talking about or of his impact.

Skeptics, unaware of the man's influence, may question the plausibility of my statement; I suggest that they listen to the recordings of the great Fletcher Henderson orchestras of the middle twenties, for they eloquently demonstrate the concept, soul, and verve of Jimmy Harrison. (I particularly recommend his solos on *Whiteman Stomp.*)

During his short-lived career, Jim graced the bandstands of not only Henderson, but also Elmer Snowden, Chick Webb, Billy Fowler, and Charlie Johnson. I recall the tug of war that Duke Ellington waged with Snowden over Jimmy's services. Neither won—Johnson finally got him. I also recall well how musicians

from all over New York City flocked into Small's Paradise nightly
to hear him and to learn the way to swing a trombone.

Jack Teagarden, the trombone volcano from Vernon, Texas,
was among the musicians who came to hear. While he owed nothing of his original style to Harrison, he was certainly later influenced by Jimmy's horn. I am not belittling in any way the
unparalleled artistry of Jack. Both he and Jimmy were strong individualists, and I get shivers up my spine when I think what a
great team they would have made. History, because of Jim Crow,
really missed a musical notation of incalculable value, since
these giants, who often jammed together, were never permitted to
play in an orchestra together or even record together.

Today, the closest replica to the Harrison sound may be heard
in Benny Morton's playing. And at times Vic Dickenson recalls
the line. In the past, Sandy Williams swung a real Harrison type
of trombone, as have Abe Lincoln, Lou McGarrity, and J. C.
Higginbotham, among others.

But over and above these musicians in whose styles one can
hear traces of Harrison, he has influenced the way jazz trombone
is played today. Previously, the trombone was used as an accompanying instrument, mostly employing smears. Jimmy's concept
was to swing it as a trumpet, thereby greatly increasing the scope
and solo potential of the trombone.

Harrison cut quite a figure when he descended upon New York.
That was back in 1923 or '24. I can't be positive about the year,
since it was so long ago, but, then, the exact year doesn't matter.
However, it is of more than passing importance that Jimmy arrived when he did, because the jazz scene was ripe for his kind
of enrichment.

I never shall forget the first time I laid eyes on him. It happened
on a balmy summer afternoon. The corner of 135th Street and
Lenox Avenue was crowded with the usual throng of musicians
who customarily hung out there, plus a cross section of night-
lifers, vaudevillians, race-horse men, and sports who, as a rule,
were never seen on the Turf in broad daylight (the Turf meant
the area bounded by the block that extended from Lenox Avenue
to Fifth Avenue and also ran south to 133rd Street).

Every head turned as two tall, sharply dressed look-a-likes promenaded into view, immaculate in Harris tweed suits with caps to match. Lips were buzz-buzzing and eyes questioned, "Who are these guys?" None of the younger fellows who were my cronies knew them, but they created so much excitement as they sauntered into the elegant Touraine Restaurant (where all the monied gentry and their ladies dined) that I slunk in behind them even though I was unaccustomed to that exalted atmosphere.

Luckily, I found a spot at the counter, and, over coffee and pie, I proceeded to watch with great curiosity as the various entertainers and musicians paused to chat at the strangers' table. Florence Mills, Dancing Dotson, Johnny Dunn, and Battle Ax (famed drummer of Jim Europe's band) were among the people who greeted the fellows, so I knew they had to be big-timers.

Then, my ears really perked up as James P. Johnson, the famous pianist and composer of *Carolina Shout* and *Keep Off the Grass* (very popular ragtime hits), entered the restaurant, looked around, and rushed up to greet them, exclaiming, "Hi there, Jimmy. Whatcha know, June? Well, I see that you birds finally made the Apple. Where are you staying? Man, wait until these New York cats hear what you can do on those horns!" Then, turning to the Lion, Willie Smith, said, "Willie, these are the bimbos that I told you I heard out in the Windy City, and you can bet a man that they can get off on them horns and blow a 'Boston' that will swing you into bad health" (a Boston was a real get-off). He continued, "Meet June Clark, trumpet man, and his sidekick, Big Jim Harrison, whose trombone makes the whores moan."

That news spread through town like wildfire, and for the next few nights there were cutting sessions all around Harlem, as the local trombonists tried to cut Jimmy down to size—but to no avail. The Toledo Terror was too much. Jimmy didn't have it all that easy, since there were lots of good trombonists around, ready and willing to test out any stranger's skill.

New York had guys like Jake Frazier, Herb Flemming, Troy Floyd, Jake Green, Teroy Williams, and Charlie Green, who was the king until Jimmy arrived. Then there were the young Turks —Charlie Irvis, Tricky Sam Nanton, and Billy Kato from New Jersey, plus Herb Gregory, a real swinger from Newark, New Jersey. Besides these fellows, there were also Abe Lincoln and Miff Mole, who played real tough. They all made the scene, coming all the way uptown to learn this new swing style.

Harrison was a genial, tall (about six feet two), well-built man. He had a big chest and long, spindly legs. His moon-shaped face and features were rather broad, and his coloration was a blend of café au lait with just enough saffron highlights to remind an onlooker of a Chinese man. As a matter of fact, Harvey Boone, who played saxophone with Henderson while we were at Connie's Inn, used to call Jimmy the Chinese Bandit. But this resemblance was quickly dispelled as soon as he opened his mouth, and you heard that Kentucky drawl.

Born in Louisville, Kentucky, in 1900, Harrison was reared in Detroit, and at an early age displayed considerable talent for music via tissue paper and comb, but he soon lost interest in music, and his after-school activities turned to baseball, which he played all through high school. I was told by saxophonist Milton Senior that Jimmy played such sterling first base that he went on tour with a local semipro team and never returned to finish high school. This was in Toledo, Ohio, to which the Harrison family migrated and opened a restaurant catering to show folks, sporting characters, and other night people. Along with solid home cooking, the Harrisons' specialty was pies, and Jimmy became the official pie-maker, which caused him to become a favorite with the clientele. In later years, he loved to boast about his cooking ability, and he would spend hours talking about recipes.

At the family restaurant, it seems, Jimmy was in charge of all the baking. He also loved to eat his pies, which posed the problem of how not to eat up the profits along with them. He and papa Harrison apparently got into several hassels over what happened to that succulent apple or strawberry pie, and Jimmy, who by that time had taken up trombone, left the restaurant. He packed up his trombone and left town with a carnival. His first job with the show was in front of the olio, a form of minstrelsy. His specialty was imitating Bert Williams.

After the carnival, the picture is vague. I've never met anyone who could fill me in on what he did professionally. I do recall his saying that he and June Clark met on the road and took to each other. They were together in many places, including Chicago, for some time. Later, they traveled to New York with either Gonzella White or the Dave and Tressie duo, or perhaps it was Joe Bright's Company (all of whom I'd seen at the Blue Mouse Theater in Washington, D.C., when my mother played piano there).

Arriving in New York, June and Jimmy graced Small's Sugar Cane on Fifth Avenue for quite some time. They were exempt from the standard procedure of being blown off their gig by some enterprising bunch of fellow musicians, as was the custom in the days before the musicians' union accepted Negro players. (Here I must qualify, to the extent of saying that I may be mistaken, and perhaps there were some Negro members of the union, but I cannot remember any, nor do I recall any attempt to gather us into the fold until years later, when I joined Fletcher Henderson.) In any case, the usual method of getting a job then was to descend upon a joint en masse and, one by one, get up on the bandstand and outblow the occupants until you got the crowd with you. The boss never failed to ask you if you wanted to work. When the originally employed musicians saw this happening, they knew that was their last night.

This was the scene all around town. At that time, there were no auditions or tryouts. Every tub had to stand on its own bottom. With the exception of that red-hot team of Jimmy and June.

I saw a lot of action and was learning a lot by sitting in at the Sugar Cane until I left town with my buddy, Happy Caldwell, for Asbury Park, New Jersey, where we became stranded. Luckily, Bobby Brown, who had a band in Newark, rescued us. After a year or so of playing in Newark, Happy and I went up to Harlem to buy some King Oliver records so we could hear Louis Armstrong.

On the corner, we ran into Harrison and were amazed to learn that he and June had split up. Jimmy was now playing at the Balconnades Ballroom with Elmer Snowden, whom I had known and idolized back home in Washington, D.C. Jimmy, while consuming ten or twelve hot dogs, told me that I could get a job with Snowden, who was looking for a trumpet player. I was reluctant, however, because there would be no spot for Happy. The tenor man with Snowden was Prince Robinson, who was next to Coleman Hawkins at that time.

However, my admiration for Jimmy's playing was great enough to overcome my hesitancy to part with Happy, and I soon joined Snowden at the Balconnades (this place was located around Sixty-sixth at Broadway and has long since disappeared). In the band were Walter Johnson, drums; Freddie Johnson, piano (no relation to Walter); Bobby Ysagurri, bass horn; Joe Garland, alto and baritone saxophones; Robinson, clarinet and tenor saxophone; and Snowden, soprano saxophone and banjo-mandolin. Jimmy's trombone and my cornet completed the lineup. I might mention that Pops Snowden had me doubling on soprano saxophone after he found out that I had previously played tenor with the Musical Spillers.

The move to Snowden's band proved to be of great value in later years, both to me and Harrison. Neither of us had been exposed to Dixieland music before, but since the ballroom featured bands such as the Original Memphis Five, the New Orleans Five, etc., we latched onto the idiom to the point that Snowden soon had many Dixieland tunes in his book. We had big ears and learned the tunes, which I never forgot (to the amazement of persons like Eddie Condon and other Dixielanders when I played with them years later).

It was not long after I'd got the nod from Snowden that all kinds of musical vistas opened up to me, sitting next to Daddy Long Legs' splendid trombone. Jimmy had a favorite expression he used all the time I knew him. He'd say, "Man, I'm sure petered tonight." At the time, I assumed this was just a sort of gag that he employed, maybe out of modesty. But after thinking about it a lot, I believe he actually was quite ill even then. (He died in 1931 of stomach cancer.)

Despite Harrison's continual protestations of not feeling well, he never stopped being one of the most creative, swinging musicians the world has ever known, and I am sure that the majority of his fellow musicians who had the good fortune to hear him in his prime will agree. Personality-plus also was one of his gifts. He was full of fun, easygoing, and I don't recall his ever raising his voice in anger. He was a lot like Teagarden, who never had a bad word to say about anyone either.

This reminds me of a happy memory concerning these two men. When Jack and Jimmy played together in Fletcher's band (unofficially, of course), they both broke up the house. Jimmy used to play *I Can't Give You Anything but Love* à la Louis Armstrong, and Teagarden mystified everybody by swinging *Mighty Lak a Rose* in waltz time!

Jimmy was a good example of a fellow rising above his environment. Although he had not finished high school, he seemed as knowledgeable as a college man. His scholastic scope was surprising, particularly in mathematics. He was the first man I'd known who could do intricate calculations in his head with lightning speed. He'd also amaze us by remembering baseball records and batting averages from many years back. We soon discovered not to bet him when he said something like "Ty Cobb stole X many bases in 19. . . ." His information always proved to be accurate. And when he remarked that Karl Marx said thus and so, it was best to take his word for the statement, for the public library would generally confirm whatever he said. (He was the first person I ever heard mention Karl Marx.)

Aside from Jim's skill in math and his bent toward philosophy, he was a gadget-man. He loved all sorts of things like bottle openers, miniature trains, and especially cameras. He took lousy pictures because, as a pastime, he was always fooling with the mechanism of his camera, so that the camera didn't work very well.

After his and June Clark's careers took separate paths, Jimmy's best buddy in New York was Coleman Hawkins. Bean and Jim were together all the time, and if you saw one, the other would soon show up. Still, an outsider would have thought from their constant arguments that they were deadly enemies. Actually, they were very good friends despite their rivalry in everything, including contests to see who could eat the most food, or who could take a chick from the other, or who could excite the crowd more blowing his horn.

There was one episode that we all laughed about for months. Jim bought a new Pontiac for one of the Henderson band's road tours, and Hawk, being his buddy, naturally rode along with Harrison. This tour took us as far south as Oklahoma City, and while we were returning to New York, the rear end dropped out of the Pontiac right in the heart of Jersey City.

The next night, after we had finished playing our opening at Roseland Ballroom, we came out of the building to feast our eyes on a most beautiful sight. At curbside stood a fire-engine-red Chrysler roadster, which drew all of us, including Coleman, like a magnet.

Hawk started his usual baiting of Jimmy. "See there, Jimmy," he said pointing, "now that's the kind of car a big-timer like you should own, not one of those cheap Ponties that the rear end falls out of. Ha ha." Then, not waiting for Jimmy's reply, Hawkins jumped into the car and drove off, leaving Jim and the rest of us open-mouthed that Hawk would buy a car and not even tell us.

Although I knew and worked with Jimmy for several years, other musicians have helped fill me in on his life before I knew him. Saxophonist Senior knew Jimmy back in Toledo. Even though I had known Milton from his days with McKinney's Cotton Pickers, it was not until I ran into him years later, when I was with Duke Ellington, that he filled me in on Jimmy's earlier years. He told me all about Jimmy's love of, and skill in, baseball and his flair for comedy (which I had been aware of). Milt and I reminisced about Jimmy at length, but with the passing of so many years, other things that he told me are no longer clear enough in my mind to recapitulate.

The jazz business has had its share of heroes, and also more than its share of tragic figures and, of course, clowns. To be sure, the clowns only momentarily amuse and arouse interest, and the unfortunates that the spotlight of tragedy has rested upon are given cursory sympathy before being consigned to oblivion. Apparently, it seems better to dismiss their contributions as a passing phase and their problems as a bad dream. The heroes, however, we tend to remember with affection and, from time to time, resurrect the memory of their gifts with the attendant nostalgia. To my mind, this is fitting. However, when a person of stature is denied all but a token recognition, then I feel it is time someone re-examined in depth his life and times.

History, inadvertently and unwittingly, bypassed Jim. Jazz, as an art form, was still in its infancy, and the observers who chose to comment in print about the music and the men who made it were insecure and uncertain as to the validity or significance of what they heard. The musicians themselves were no help, since no thinking, erudite tooter in the past would be caught dead reading anything other than the sport pages. This is not to imply that all musicians were too benighted or too unqualified to think, talk, and write about their music. What I am saying is that in this happy and fraternal atmosphere, the making of music was considered fun, and, in that spirit, the fellows by and large frowned upon any cerebral effort to explain their skills and way of life to the public. Among the rank and file, the thinking was: "Let 'em write—they can't play, so how can they know what they're talking about?"

This attitude was unrealistic and erroneous, as time has proved. The story of jazz can never be completed, and it explains to some degree how a person such as Jimmy Harrison has come to be almost completely ignored by historians. Too, it is unfortunate that Jimmy died so young. Born in 1900, he was barely thirty when he died, not having had the opportunity to continue displaying his talents to the world. Had he lived through the thirties and forties, then unquestionably he would have been recognized and remembered as the father of the swing trombone.

Down Beat, May 5, 1966

Coleman Hawkins, "The Father of Tenor Saxophone"

THE FIRST TIME I saw Coleman Hawkins was in 1919, and I was twelve. I particularly remember the occasion, since it was the first time I ever had gone to a theater. Mamie Smith and Her Jazz Hounds were the stars of the show at the Howard Theater, in Washington, D.C., but running her a close second in popularity was a mahogany-colored fellow who blew the house down, playing an instrument I'd never seen before. Later, I found out that the instrument was a tenor saxophone, and the slap-tonguing sensation was Coleman Hawkins. According to Hawk's latest count —which has him born in 1904—he was just fifteen then, but he looked like a man to me.

Two years later I was in New York City at the Garden of Joy, a celebrated night spot in Harlem. There, I had the experience of my young life as I heard both Hawk and Sidney Bechet, in the same band, blowing at each other.

After that high point, there was a period when I did not hear Coleman for quite a long time, and Willie Lewis (the clarinet player and my chaperone while I was with the Musical Spillers) told me that Hawk was on the road with a singer.

In any case, the next time I laid eyes on Mr. Saxophone, he was escorting a beautiful brown-skinned girl into the classiest restaurant in Harlem. It was Glenn's Restaurant, which catered only to the crème de la crème of Harlemites.

When I saw him going in there, I thought to myself that the

scuttlebutt about Hawk's playing with the biggest-time orchestra in New York—Fletcher Henderson's—must be true. They were appearing at what I was told was the first Broadway club to feature an all-colored revue of extravaganza proportions, the Plantation Club. Shortly thereafter, all Harlem was agog over the news that Fletcher had left the Plantation for the Roseland Ballroom because of Hawk's refusal to appear in the production part of the program without being compensated for the extra stint.

This move proved to be the best thing that ever could have happened for Louis Brecker (the boss of Roseland), Fletcher, and Coleman. The orchestra quickly swung its way into the hearts of the Great White Way, and Hawk was the outstanding star.

Every night was a holiday during those early days at Roseland, and the area behind the iron railing across from Henderson's bandstand was filled with people, many of them musicians, extending all the way back to the raised booth where the electrician worked the lights. Among the illustrious music lovers there on any given night might be Cole Porter, Jack (Legs) Diamond, Walter Winchell, Benny Leonard, and even New York City's mayor, Jimmy Walker. Every night after the band had finished, Coleman Hawkins was still on—the hero of the evening.

In several ways, Hawkins differs from the usual public conception of a musician. He is not the prototype of the affable extrovert. Coleman presents a dignified facade that often borders on the cool side, something that can be unnerving to people who do not know him.

Among old pals, however, he can be quite jovial and enthusiastic over something that interests him. One of his early and continuing interests is his love for fine clothes, which he wears with a flair (yet, I can recall a phase during which he would buy the most expensive garment that Ben Rocke, a favorite Broadway tailor, offered and not have it cleaned or pressed during an entire season).

After I ventured into the exalted company of the Henderson orchestra at Roseland, I really got to know the great ones in this galaxy of tremendous musicians—Hawk, altoist Don Redman, trombonist Big Charlie Green, clarinetist Buster Bailey, drummer Joe (Kaiser) Marshall, and the others.

At first, I felt very strange in Smack's band, perhaps because of the idiosyncrasies of the fellows. For instance, Big Green had to have two things with him at all times—his big pistol and a bottle of gin. Then, Coleman amazed me by consuming more food at one sitting than I had ever seen anybody else eat. Perhaps that's where he gets his tremendous energy. A typical meal for Hawk would start with ham and eggs and hot cakes, while his steak covered with onions was being prepared. The steak would not be a breakfast-size portion. It would be a full-size porterhouse, accompanied with hash browns or French fries. This snack would usually be topped off with a slab of pie and ice cream. Being both young and impressionable, I copied Hawk's eating habits with gusto, and by the time Fletcher's band had returned from our first road tour, I had gained a bit of weight, jumping from 145 to 180 in one summer.

Hawk had some other habits that seemed strange to me at the time. One of them came to my notice when we went on the road in the spring after our annual stay at Roseland. As usual, on hitting a town, we all went to look the burg over, and it so happened that I found myself with Coleman in a department store. He went to the cosmetic counter and bought several bars of a very expensive soap. Hawk's remark that this was a year's supply and a great bargain made me wonder how he could figure that six bars of soap would last him a whole year.

But the next morning in the hotel, I found out. First, out came a pair of ornate washcloths, then the special soap, then some ordinary soap. One cloth was for the special soap, the other for the ordinary, and never the twain should meet. The fancy soap was daintily applied to a corner of washcloth number one. That was for his face and around his eyes only. Then, the ordinary soap, applied to the other cloth, was used on his body. I had never seen such a production in my life. Years later, however, I came across an article on the bathing habits of the French court. Perhaps Coleman's method wasn't so odd after all.

Another facet of Mr. Saxophone's character is his frugality, and I am certain that there will never have to be a benefit given for Coleman Hawkins. I well remember in the slap-happy days of hail-fellow-well-met how we'd take over Big John's bar and each of us in turn would set up the bar for the gang. But invariably, when it came Bean's turn, something happened. He would be in the telephone booth or the men's room, or he had cut out for the evening. This is not to imply that Hawk is cheap; it's just that he is cautious. Before he got over his mistrust of banks, it was common for him to walk around with $2,000 or $3,000 in his pockets! One time, he carried with him his salary from an entire season of summer touring, about $9,000. When we became stranded, for some reason or other, Hawk laughed while showing his roll. But he wouldn't give a quarter to see the Statue of Liberty do the twist on the Brooklyn Bridge at high noon.

There was the time, however, when Coleman and his buddy, Jimmy Harrison, got their comeuppance. This was when there was a great turnover of bass players in Smack's band, and, among them, there was a fellow named Delbert Thomas. Perhaps some of the remaining old-timers around New York will recall Delbert. He was a seemingly slow-thinking person who spoke with an even slower drawl. We thought he was a real country boy, but later we understood otherwise.

This episode dates back to the days when college youngsters started hiring big bands to play for their weekend dances. Accommodations were quite a problem, and one weekend we all had to stay in a little old shacklike house on the edge of town. Because of the college curfew, the town folded up early, but we were unaccustomed to going to bed at such an hour, so we started up a few games—a blackjack operation and a poker session. Del asked to be shown how to play and then broke most of us guys in the blackjack game.

At the poker table, Smack, Jimmy, Hawk, and Buster were battling. When Delbert asked for a hand, I caught the smirk on their faces, and I felt sorry for him. The feeling was even more positive when Hawk and Jimmy started kidding him, saying that the game

was too rich for his blood and that they hated to take candy from
a baby. But Del persisted, saying that he trusted them to show
him how to play. They finally dealt him in, and needless to say,
Del won the table, leaving Jimmy broke and Hawkins badly bent.
The capper came years later when we found out that Delbert
previously had earned his living hustling three-card monte and
all the rest of the card games in a carnival.

Coleman is essentially a loner, and with the exception of Harrison, I don't know anyone with whom he was ever really close.
Although Hawk and Roy Eldridge played a lot together, somehow
they didn't seem to be with it together when off the stand. I realize that this is mostly speculation on my part, since I don't really
know, not having been on their scene most of the time. However,
I do know how close Bean and Jim were.

There was always a lot of good-natured teasing between them,
but when Jimmy bought a Pontiac, Hawk accorded him a lot
more respect than he had previously and stopped kidding Jim so
roughly. They ate together, hung out as a team, and got along
fine, until Coleman made the mistake of buying a raccoon coat,
which became the talk of Harlem. I've heard how a woman can
break up a friendship between two men, but this is the first time
I ever came across a situation in which a fur coat was the cause.

It started at one of those breakfast dances that Harlem was
noted for at the time. At the peak of the evening, Hawk made his
entrance looking like an Oriental potentate, with a beauty on each
arm. When he was seated, all the pretty little showgirls converged
upon his table, where, of course, Jimmy also was seated with his
date. The showgirls went into ecstasies, raving about Hawk's
coat. And Jimmy's date, not to be outdone, draped the garment
around herself, remarking in a loud, clear voice, "This fur piece is
the living end, and to get its twin, I, for one, would take anything
that goes along with it, including you, Coleman."

I'm sure she was only joking, but by a strange coincidence, two
weeks later she was sporting a coat that looked exactly like
Hawk's. Jimmy looked rather glum for a spell. I don't know if it
was poetic justice or not, but only a few months later Coleman's
raccoon went up in smoke. It caught on fire from the exhaust pipe

that heated the bus we were using to make a series of one-night-ers.

Hawk's flair for clothes is one of the striking aspects of the man, and this has been evident since that first time I saw him. On that occasion, he was wearing bell-bottom trousers and what was called in 1919 a shimmy-back coat. I expect him to deny wearing any such garment, but that was high style in those days.

As a youngster, Hawkins was very fond of sports and knew all the batting averages and pitching records by heart and, as a matter of fact, baseball appeared to be his consuming interest. But you could have knocked us all over with a feather when Coleman came out to play baseball on one of those rare occasions when we were all sober enough to think it would be fun. I still chuckle over it.

The Hendersons had been challenged by some other band when we were playing at the Southland Club in Boston, Massachusetts. The game was to be played with regulation equipment, hard ball, etc. Smack was the starting pitcher and did pretty well for an inning or so. Then Jimmy Harrison left first base to take over the pitching chores.

Just then, a weird sight ambled across Boston Common. I looked, blinking my eyes from left field, at the spectacle of a fellow wearing a panama hat, tuxedo, and patent-leather shoes, Coleman Hawkins' uniform for participating in the national pastime. The ensemble was set off by an even funnier note—the tender way he carried a new first baseman's mitt.

When he announced that we were in the presence of the world's greatest shortstop, Jimmy laughed until tears came to his eyes and said, "Hawk, that's a first baseman's mitt you've got there." This made Coleman quite indignant, and he replied, "Any damn fool knows that, Stringbeans, but I've got to protect these valuable fingers or *you* won't eat." So, to keep peace, Fletcher put Bean in at shortstop. Batter up. And the first ball was hit right to Hawk. He fielded the ball, threw the man out, stuck his mitt into his hip pocket, and walked off the field. That was the end of Coleman's baseball career, as far as I know.

Hawk was not just bragging when he spoke of his valuable

fingers, since his inspired tenor saxophone playing began to make history as it sparked Smack's band. Roseland started doing capacity business as a result of presenting the first really down-home swinging colored band. It differed from Piron's Creole Orchestra, a more sedate group of musicians from New Orleans who had previously played the spot. So Fletcher hit Broadway just at the right time for the dancing public.

At that time, the only rival in the group that could come close to competing with Hawk for the crowd's favor was Big Charlie Green, an ex-carnival trombonist from Omaha, Nebraska. Green, a six-footer, was a beautiful instrumentalist with perfect command of his horn, and his playing ran from very sweet to a braying, raucous shouting style.

Bean used to cool Charlie's horn off whenever he wanted to by saying to Buster Bailey or Don Redman, in Green's hearing, "Well, I guess I'd better call my old lady. It's not that I don't trust her, but I want her to know that I'm thinking about her." This remark never failed to upset Green, who was a jealous husband, and when he got upset, he'd hit his gin bottle. As the evening drew on, Charlie's playing grew sadder and sadder. Yet, he never seemed to realize that Hawk planned it that way. They called it "signifying" in those days.

If there is any validity in my feeling that a sense of humor is a prime requisite in music, then many things about Coleman Hawkins become clear. In him we have a person who, despite his facade, actually enjoys life but paradoxically goes to great lengths to conceal his enjoyment and even his admiration for the work of others. He especially enjoys putting people on. Both in print and in recorded interviews, he seldom has a good word for his peers. You may question Hawk for an opinion about anyone from Duke Ellington to Louis Armstrong, and the best you can expect is some kind of derogatory remark or a grunt, which may indicate anything or nothing. Then, later he has been heard gleefully telling how he fooled someone again.

There's also the preoccupation Bean has always had with age. As far back as I can remember, he would kid Jimmy or Don about how much older they were than he, and this was in the twenties,

mind you. As recently as the forties, in the war years, when I ran
into Hawk in Chicago, he was still at it, bemoaning the fact that
his mean old draft board had reclassified him 1-A. Then, pulling
out a draft card that gave his age as thirty-five (the draft limit at
that time), he continued to rave on, cussing out General Louis
Hershey, the draft board, and himself for being unfortunate
enough to be so young. Roy Eldridge looked at me, and I looked
at Roy, both of us thinking the same thought—who's he kidding?
Then John Kirby said, "Damn, Bean, if you keep getting younger,
you'll have to start wearing diapers again."

On the plus side, there are the many facets of Hawk's talent.
He plays the piano beautifully, though not in public. I have sat,
unknown to him, enthralled for hours as he rhapsodized at the
keyboard. I'm sure he'll never figure out when this took place.
Then, too, Hawk is a fine arranger, but few people would ever
guess it. I remember well the splendid scores he made for Henderson while he was in the band. Of course, it took him about two
years to come up with *Singing in the Rain* and another gem, the
name of which I've forgotten, and there was also a wonderful
ballad he composed and arranged that was so great Smack used
it for a theme song on our network broadcasts from Connie's Inn.

There's another dimension to this extraordinary man of music,
which has to do with his almost superhuman strength on his instrument. This is not to say that brute strength could be considered a prerequisite for greatness. However, this feat impressed
me so much that it bears repeating. Fletcher, en route from Kentucky to Detroit, rousted me out of bed in Cincinnati (I was in
the Queen City working with his brother, Horace) and told me
that there'd been an auto accident that left him short two trumpet
players and that I was to be a replacement until they rejoined
him. Most important of all, the job that night was to be a battle
of bands between McKinney's Cotton Pickers and Smack's outfit
in the Greystone Ballroom in Detroit. As we burned up the familiar road between Cincy and the Motor City, I wondered who
would play the first trumpet book, since Russell Smith had been
one of those injured.

On arrival, we set up and, much to my surprise, Coleman—on

tenor—took over the first trumpet book and not only played the parts so well that we scarcely missed the first trumpet but also carried the orchestra with volume such as I had never heard coming out of a tenor sax. And the Greystone was a huge place!

Speaking of Bean's prowess reminds me of the three distinct changes in his playing that I've noticed over the years. First, the slap-tongue effect. Then, later, when we played Toledo, Ohio, Hawk, like the rest of us, was greatly impressed by a young fellow named Art Tatum, who displayed such a wealth of talent on the piano. His then-new conception of anticipating the chord changes within the framework of a tune left us numb from the experience. But on leaving Toledo, we overlooked the significance of what we'd heard.

Months later, Bean put this approach on record, making several sides with the Mound City Blue Blowers, and a new style was born, as New York went crazy over *Hello, Lola* and *If I Could Be With You One Hour Tonight.*

The third change became evident in a rather humorous way and took place after Coleman returned to New York after four or five years in Europe. There, his international image grew considerably as a result of being featured with Jack Hylton, who led the most prestigious orchestra in Europe at that time.

Even before he returned, many stories were being told around the bars where we hung out. Hawk, it was rumored, had a chalet in Switzerland and was retired; another story had a certain Spanish countess committing suicide over the loss of his affections. The most-repeated rumor was that Coleman had decided to live out the rest of his life abroad, rather than return to Jim Crow. But despite all the talk, return he did, and unveiled a third style—an extension of the earlier, Tatum-influenced approach but with a difference. Now, Hawk punctuated more, and he often employed in contrast such a continuous flow of changing chords that people marveled at his control and stamina. He was still too much for every tub on that horn, it subsequently turned out.

However, the prelude to the unveiling of these new effects was an incident that will be recalled with amusement by everybody who was on the scene. Nightsy Johnson, a drummer, had opened a small joint catering to musicians only, and that's where the hippies hung out. I can see in retrospect that Billie Holiday's favorite tenor sax man and his followers really made the place. Lester Young was the man, and it didn't hurt business when the news got around that Lady Day could be seen there almost every night. The location was 134th Street and Saint Nicholas Avenue, a basement club, and the pad was always bad.

But then the word spread like wildfire: Bean was back! Hawk started falling into the joint every night, immaculate, sophisticated, and saxophoneless. The tension continued to build—is this the night he will play? Coleman just sat there sipping, with a smirk on his face, as they all paraded their talents before him. And, from time to time, they all had their innings—Illinois Jacquet, Chu Berry, Don Byas, Dick Wilson, and so on—all leading tenor men. Then came the second-liners, tooters like Julian Dash, Big Nick Nicholas, Bob Carroll, and Elmer Williams, while Hawk still sat and sipped, evidently enjoying the drama he was creating. The sight of the comrades ensconced all over the place reminded me of a bunch of vultures, waiting and licking their chops in absorbed anticipation of fattening up their reputations on Coleman.

Finally, the great event took place. Hawk fell in later than usual —it was about 3:00 A.M.—and as luck would have it, Lady Day was singing, which rarely happened uptown in those days (1939). Of course, Lester accompanied her. Bean strode in, unpacked his axe and joined them, to everybody's surprise. Then, when Billie finished, she announced to the house that it had been a pleasure to have had the world's greatest tenor saxophonist backing her up —Lester Young!

You could have heard a pin drop after that remark, but the Hawk ignored it, turning to the piano player and saying, "Play me a few choruses of—." I've forgotten the name of the tune, but I do recall that the tempo Hawk set was almost unbelievable, it was so fast. And he had the tune all to himself.

Then, he sauntered to the bar, had a big drink, and waited to see how the cats would follow this avalanche of virtuosity. For some reason, nobody felt like blowing at the moment. So Coleman picked up where he had left off, this time with a ballad, in which he proceeded to demonstrate the various ways the tune could be embellished, finishing up with an incredible cadenza, to thundering applause. He then gallantly started toying with *Honeysuckle Rose,* motioning for Chu and Don Byas to join him, which they did.

Lester sat on the sidelines, drinking with Lady Day, and I must say that he kept his cool. This I know, because I, along with everybody else, was watching Lester to see how he reacted. And after Bean again took charge of the situation on *Honeysuckle,* guys started leaving, and I heard Dick Wilson say to Elmer Williams, "Well, that's that. Coleman is still the boss, and when you tangle with him, you'd better know what you're doing or you'd better ask somebody."

Down Beat, May 19, 1966

Red Norvo: A Tale of a Pioneer

RED NORVO is a self-effacing man and always has been. It may even be that of the multitude of vibraharp players who have come on the jazz scene in recent years there are a couple who don't know his name and wouldn't recognize him if he walked in on a Milt Jackson recording session.

Whether this situation can be attributed to Red's disinterest in blowing his own horn or to contemporary jazz historians' disinterest in blowing it for him is a matter for quibbling, but that he deserves a niche in jazz' panoply of great players is beyond dispute because he is one of the trail-blazers.

He came by his degree from the school of jazz honestly, incubating in Chicago's south side and New York City's Harlem. But he had quite a way to go before he graduated. He started in the bucolic atmosphere of Beardstown, Illinois, where he was born in 1908.

One spring, a flood caused great damage to Beardstown, so young Kenneth Norville was sent to Rolla, Missouri, to stay with his two brothers, who were attending a state school of mines, until the flood subsided. While there, he found his life's work. In the local vaudeville pit orchestra there was a drummer-xylophone player named Wentwood. Red was fascinated with his playing and hung around until Wentwood invited him to try the xylophone when the theater was closed. Red loved every minute of the few lessons Wentwood gave him.

As Red tells it, from then on, he would go to sleep dreaming of the instrument and could hardly eat for longing for the day when he'd own a xylophone. After returning to Beardstown, he worked all summer, saving his earnings. When he learned that the total he had saved did not add up to nearly enough to buy his dream, he decided to relinquish his most prized possession, a pony. The pet was sold for $135—exactly the sum that would enable him to buy the only xylophone in town. Kenneth Norville was on his way.

But it wasn't an easy or an obvious way for a third-generation Scot born and reared in a rural section of the country where there was small exposure to popular music. His family clung to the square dance, folk songs, and such fare as was presented on the chautauqua circuit. There was talent in the family. Papa Norville played the violin, mama accompanied on the organ, and young Kenneth was soon able to join the family group. Aside from this contact with music in his home, there were infrequent visits to vaudeville theaters (which were not encouraged by Red's parents), and the school orchestra. Red, with his flaming hair, good looks, and talent on the unorthodox xylophone attracted the little girls in droves.

Among them were two girl friends who played violin, loved to sing, and enjoyed harmonizing on the tunes of the day. Red joined them, and the threesome lived for music. They performed in a modified, free-wheeling style that the conservative director of the school band deplored. However, they were popular around Beardstown, playing picnics and school dances. Then, the trio was invited to play a summer engagement in Chicago!

Red recalls his reluctance to leave home. He just wasn't for it, until he realized how much he would hate to stop playing with his chums. There was no one else in town comparable to les girls and then, too, there was all that money and an opportunity to see the big city. So off they went.

At the close of the engagement, the girls returned home. But Red stayed on. By that time, Norvo knew where he was going, and it was not back home.

There were days of scuffling around Chicago with hit-and-miss club dates and then unexpectedly an offer to join a new group that was in rehearsal, calling themselves the Collegians. It consisted of six marimba players!

Red almost missed out on this because he didn't think he was good enough to play with the combo, but they talked him into joining. With the addition of Red's xylophone, it became a seven-man crew, a rather large group. Still, they worked steadily. Jobs, in those times, were no problem. There were not enough good bands to go around, with the demand in clubs, dance halls, vaudeville theaters, and burlesque houses. The same situation existed in all the major cities. The demand exceeded the supply of good musicians.

When Norvo joined the Collegians, the move proved to have far-reaching consequences, because it was through them that he was introduced to the south side musical atmosphere. At the time, this was the finishing school for everyone who admired jazz and wanted to learn how to play like the originators. On the south side, Red heard the brothers Johnny and Baby Dodds, King Oliver, Earl Hines, Jimmie Noone, and others too numerous to mention. The area was jumping, and one of its prime movers was drummer Jasper Taylor, who also beat big rhythm on washboard and improvised stomp choruses on what was known in those days as drummer's bells or orchestra bells. (I can remember seeing Kaiser Marshall, Fletcher Henderson's drummer, use this instrument to change keys in an arrangement.)

After leaving the Collegians, Red played as a single in vaudeville. Today, he laughs as he recalls playing the *Poet and Peasant* overture and closing his act with a tap dance. About that time, he became known as Red Norvo. His name was changed by accident. Paul Ash, who led the band at the Oriental Theater, had trouble remembering the last syllable of Red's name. It would come out Norwood or Norbert. One day he pronounced it "Norvo," a *Variety* reviewer wrote up Red's act using that name, and everybody advised Red to stick with it.

After this adventure into the two-a-day branch of show biz

(which sometimes turned out to be three and four a day), Red concluded that this was not the life for him. The time was not right for a jazz xylophone player, no matter how gifted, but another opportunity came his way. Victor Young, the composer-conductor, approached him with an offer from NBC where he'd get a chance at all kinds of music as a radio staff man in various size groups. Red jumped at the chance and remained with Young until going east with Paul Whiteman, with whom he had worked in the studio.

Thanks to the musical grapevine, Red did not arrive in New York as a stranger. His reputation had preceded him, and I was glad to meet him when Adrian Rollini (the world's greatest bass saxophonist) took Red up to Harlem. In those days, Harlem was the section where the musical action was, the eastern counterpart of Chicago's south side. After every other place in town had closed, the uptown joints started jumping, with a cross-section of Broadway show people, musicians, thugs, and dance-happy people in attendance. Among the night-lifers there'd be musicians who later became famous. The Dorseys, Bix, Eddie Lang, Miff Mole, trombonist George Troupe, Bunny Berigan, Bud Freeman, Rollini, and Red made the rounds of Harlem at least once a week. But we never had a chance to hear Red play, because there were no xylophones in Harlem.

If memory serves, Red began to record on his own in that era (1933), along with his gig with Whiteman. But he might as well have been playing on Mars or Jupiter for all the good it did us uptowners. We couldn't find the records, and we couldn't get into any of the spots where Whiteman was appearing. In those days there was a definite Jim Crow attitude. Downtown night clubs had a strict "white only" policy. Because of the existing situation, it was a miracle that I got to hear Norvo as early in his career as I did. These were the circumstances:

One afternoon, when we were lolling around the Rhythm Club, my roomie (saxophonist Happy Caldwell) and my buddy (trumpeter Ward Pinkett) decided that the club was too noisy and that what our nerves required was some soothing syrup. So we went around the corner to Big John's saloon in search of peace and quiet, and with the avowed purpose of seeing which one of us would be able to stand up longest under that lethal brew, a popular Harlem drink called "top 'n' bottom," made of gin and port wine. I guess the fact that it was snowing like Faust had a lot to do with our mood for the sauce, although in those days nobody required any excuse for drinking.

No sooner had we racked back a round or two than the door burst open, and guitarist Bernard Addison (who incidentally gave me my first pair of long pants) skidded up to where we were sitting, exclaiming excitedly, "Good God Almighty! I've just returned from Patterson, New Jersey, and I heard something that you won't believe. I played a gig there last night, and this afternoon, on the way to the train station, I saw 'Paul Whiteman, the King of Jazz' on a theater marquee. Ha ha, heh heh, ha ha ha ha."

We knew why Bernard was laughing so hard, because to us Harlemites, Pops' outfit didn't come near to being a jazz band, no matter what his press agent said. This is not to say that Whiteman didn't have the greatest dance orchestra in the land, but you couldn't truthfully call it a jazz band.

Bernard continued, "I fell into this theater just in time to hear Red Norvo on his xylophone—the kind of mess that sounded like one of the cats who had been raised on the corner of 135th Street and Fifth Avenue!"

This was a phenomenon, since in the early twenties, when the downtown brothers first began to enter the dance-band field, it was a rare thing to hear them keep steady beat going from start to finish of a tune. To our ears, their solo efforts were equally inept. I don't mean to denigrate the few white groups who really successfully emulated the originators, nor those certain rare individuals in a class by themselves.

In any case, Bernie's statement caused an uproar. Most of the players took it as a big joke, until a few of the older fellows, like trumpeter Joe Smith and trombonist Big Charlie Green, told us that you can't judge a book by its cover and not to be too sure that we were the only ones who could swing. These remarks infuriated us, and right then we decided to find out for ourselves.

I recall that it was snowing as if God wanted to get this blizzard

over in a hurry, but that didn't stop us. We fortified ourselves
with spare half-pints and headed for Patterson. Braving the rigors
of the weather, we took a streetcar down to the 125th Street ferry
dock, boarded the ferry, continued through Hackensack via streetcar, transferred to a second streetcar and then to a third damn
streetcar.

Finally we arrived at the theater where Whiteman's band was
appearing. Featured in the band, sure enough, was a swinging
xylophone player named Red Norvo. Red was only given the solo
spot on one or two numbers in the stage show, as I recall, but that
was enough to set our hearts thumping and our heads nodding in
agreement. This cat had it!

The news spread quickly all over Harlem. Once we were convinced, we always brought up Norvo's name whenever somebody
said ofays couldn't swing. From that first time I heard Red, I
could see how he belonged in a big-time orchestra like Pops
Whiteman's, because he made them swing when he soloed, just
as Bix Beiderbecke had done.

While Red and singer Mildred Bailey were members of the
Whiteman entourage, romance blossomed and led to marriage.
After Red had led his own octet at the Hickory House on Fifty-
second Street, he and Mildred decided to form their own big orchestra, which they did successfully, hiring musicians who not
only showed great promise but who also were compatible. The
list of chaps who played in this band reads like a *Who's Who* of
jazz, and the book was studded with early efforts by arranger
Eddie Sauter.

One of the luckiest records for "Mr. and Mrs. Swing," as they
became known, was a tune called *Weekend of a Private Secretary*,
which was a big hit. It was one of the first big-band efforts that
employed the enthusiastic Latin rhythm throughout. After a few
good years with the band, the war intervened, and transportation
hassles, along with ever-changing personnel, caused the great
group to fold. Also, somewhere along the line, Mr. and Mrs. Swing
became incompatible and were divorced.

Red still speaks warmly of Mildred. Although he concedes that she was temperamental, he explained that Mildred was really two people. One was a warm, solicitous wife and the other a moody, excitable artist. After their breakup, Mildred appeared as a solo artist until her death in 1951, while Red also went his own way, first with his own group and later with Benny Goodman. In 1943, he made the switch from xylophone to vibraharp. Red later married Eve Rogers, trumpeter Shorty Rogers' sister, and they have three children, Mark (now twenty-four), Portia nineteen, and Kevin sixteen.

Red was featured with Woody Herman's band in 1946, settled in California in 1947, and in 1949 came back east to lead an all-star sextet. The following year, he formed a trio with guitarist Tal Farlow and Charlie Mingus on bass (later Jimmy Raney and Red Mitchell).

Except for a stint with Benny Goodman in 1959, Red continued to front his own combos, often working in Las Vegas, where he has also led hotel house bands and teamed up, on occasion, with Frank Sinatra.

In appearance, Red today looks like a well-preserved Norseman. The once flaming hair is muted with gray, and he sports a beard. His face projects a rare, sympathetic, almost benign understanding of mankind. A pixie glint of devilry emanates from his steel-blue eyes when he laughs, as he often does. It is the eyes that reveal the inner man—a sincere person, a gentleman who commands respect both for his music and himself.

While reminiscing recently, Red recalled many vignettes. There was the time, during his last few years with Whiteman, that he buddied with Bix, who roomed with singer Harry Barris at the Hotel Forrest. Roy Wilson, a mutual friend who was also staying in the hotel, rented a piano. The fellows used to congregate in Roy's room to hear Bix rhapsodize at the piano. Red remembers Bix as an extremely gifted musician and a very gentle person.

There was the curious story about Adrian Rollini. Back in the twenties, Rollini was *the* bass saxophone player. Then came his friendship with Norvo and exposure to the new vibraharp. To the amazement of everybody in the business, Rollini dropped the saxophone and went on to play the vibraharp exclusively for the rest of his life. Today, his widow, Dixie Rollini, handcrafts special vibraharp mallets for Red.

One of Red's most astonished moments came during a stage show. The pit orchestra began a fanfare for him and as the curtains opened, Norvo was aghast to see his xylophone ascending toward the ceiling. The instrument had become entangled in the curtain. . . .

Red cherishes memories of the glamor of being featured with Whiteman; the excitement when he was leader on his own early record dates with all-star groups including such names as Artie Shaw, Bunny Berigan, Chu Berry, Jack Jenny, Teddy Wilson, Gene Krupa, and Charlie Barnet (significantly, most of these fellows later became famous bandleaders); the days of Mr. and Mrs. Swing; and the happy period when he was a member of Benny Goodman's famed sextet.

Red has become philosophic over the years. When we spoke of the contemporary scene, he did not put anybody down, but he said he deeply regrets the lack of historical truth in the chronicling of jazz and the ignoring and/or stifling of creativity by big business. He also deplores what he feels is the even more disastrous prevailing attitude that exists among many of the musicians who say they must express themselves and the public be damned.

"Of course, to themselves, perhaps, they are saying something," he said, "but the audience who pays the freight is entitled to pleasure in return . . . and they are rapidly getting out of the habit of listening."

To prove his point, he noted that the clubs that were the showcases for the avant-garde are rapidly disappearing, the youngsters flocking instead to their own kind of clubs, where the talent is not overpriced. "The only remaining hope for a creative musical America exists in such settings that the young people can afford and where they derive pleasure," Red said.

These days, Red works with his quartet as much as he chooses, playing such places as Chicago's London House, New York's Rainbow Grill, and Los Angeles' Century Plaza. These engagements are sandwiched between appearances at Lake Tahoe and Las Vegas in Nevada, and, most recently, at the Newport Jazz Festival.

Red's contribution (over and above his being consistently one of the most gifted and communicative players on the vibraharp) lies in the fact that he singlehandedly made the xylophone sound a part of the lexicon of swing. Without question, he must be categorized as a charter member of that select group—the innovators —whom the profession considers immortals.

Down Beat, September 7, 1967

The Days With Duke

THERE IS NO GREATER NAME in musical Americana than that of
Duke Ellington, who, over several decades, has innovated,
created, and dignified American music with such skill and devotion that his name has become synonymous with the best of the
art form.

Ellington's prolific pen has provided such imaginative scores,
and the presentation of himself and his orchestra has been so ur-
bane and sophisticated, that he is the obvious subject of reams of
stories and interviews. But strangely enough, very little is known
of his thoughts and dreams—the inside workings of Duke as a human being. This is not to imply that I know Duke better than anyone else, but I do feel that I have a different frame of reference
from most people's. At various times I have been his barber, chef,
valet, third trumpet man in his orchestra, and his poker opponent.
From where I sit, Ellington fits the description of an iceberg:
there's much more beneath the surface than above.

Our initial meeting was unforgettable, at least for me. The
scene was Washington, D.C., where we both lived in the north-
west section. One hot summer day when I was fooling around the
pool at the YMCA (where I had no business, since I couldn't
swim), I slipped and fell in. It would have been curtains for Stewart that day, but an older fellow pulled me out. Edward Kennedy

Ellington was my lifesaver, and though he has forgotten the incident (and in fact swears that he can't swim), I well remember his rescuing me.

The next time our paths crossed there was an event we both remember with much amusement. It was at Odd Fellows Hall in Georgetown, where there was always a dance on Saturday night. A lot of us youngsters used to hang around the hall, peeping in the windows at the dancers and musicians. This particular Saturday night there was a quartet working that sounded great to us kids because they played the popular tunes of the day, such as *It's Right Here for You, and If You Don't Get It, It's No Fault of Mine; Walking the Dog; He May Be Your Man, But He Comes to See Me Sometime.* We gaped over the fence, drinking in the bright lights, the pretty girls, the festive atmosphere, and the good music.

Suddenly, I yelled to my buddy, "Hey, that guy playing piano —I know him. That's Eddie Ellington!" And so it was. Although it was a small band, they sounded mellow, especially the leader, Tobin, who was playing the sax, an instrument we had never heard before. Duke was on piano, Otto Hardwicke on bass fiddle, and there was a drummer they called Stickamackum.

These dances always started sedately, but as the night wore on and the liquor flowed faster, the tougher element went into action, and the customary fight erupted. This time it was a real brawl, and the Georgetown toughs ran the band out of the hall.

Everyone took off but the drummer. Sticks just pulled his switch-blade knife and said, "I don't go nowhere without my drums, an' if you want to fight me, go right ahead. But touch them drums, an' somebody's got to die." Evidently they believed him because while the other fellows in the band were hotfooting it down Twenty-ninth Street (with Duke in the lead), old Sticks just sat there chewing his tobacco unmolested.

A few years later, I got to know Duke better. At that time, I was rehearsing with a kid band. Our leader hung out on the corner of Seventh and T streets, which was *the* hangout for Washington musicians then. By tagging along, I got to see all the local big-timers—Doc Perry, Elmer Snowden, Sam Taylor, Gertie Wells, Claude Hopkins, and many others. Eddie Ellington had already acquired the nickname Duke by this time, and he, too, hung out on the corner. In fact, he had the added distinction of being "king" of Room Ten in True Reformers Hall, which stood on the same corner. Room Ten was where the teenagers held their get-togethers. I can still see young Ellington playing the piano and fixing that famous hypnotic smile on the nearest pretty girl.

In spite of knowing Duke so long and so well, I almost missed out playing with his band. After we all landed in New York City, although I wasn't the only one he thought would enhance his group (he and Elmer Snowden carried on a tug-of-war over the services of Prince Robinson, who was about the best clarinet and tenor sax man in the city), it became almost a habit with him to ask me to join the band. But I never took him up on his offers. For one thing, I was playing with Fletcher Henderson's band, which I loved, and for another, I had no eyes for the Jungle Band and all that growling mess. During the seven or so years I played with Henderson, we got a kick out of catching Duke's band in a ballroom battle of bands because our shouting, fast tempos always overpowered Duke's more subtle, original efforts.

It was after I left Henderson and struck out on my own for a brief period that the chain of circumstances began that led me into the Ellington band. Irving Mills, who was Duke's manager at the time, caught my group at the Empire Ballroom and suggested I do a small-band record date for him. The date did not materialize for some time; meanwhile, my band folded, and I joined Luis Russell. After I finally did the record date, I went to Mills' office to collect my check and ran into Duke. There was the usual musicians' repartee when all of a sudden Duke fixed me with that hypnotic grin and said, "Fat Stuff, it's just about time you came home. Join my band!" Mills tried to convince me, too, but I still didn't feel I would be happy with the band. Then when they told me the salary was seventy-five dollars a week, I laughed and walked out. Depression or no, I had been earning as much as $125 a week.

When I arrived home later, I heard Jonesy, Duke's band boy, yelling up the stairs to my wife on the second floor, "Tell Rex to come down and get fitted for uniforms."

I was not the only one astonished by these words, having just refused the job. Standing in my doorway talking to my wife was Luis Russell's drummer, who gaped open-mouthed at Jonesy and dashed down the stairs past me. Apparently he rushed right down to Russell with the news that I was going to leave him and join Duke because that night on the job as I started to unpack my horn, Russell said, "Pack it up. You're fired. I've already got your replacement."

So, jobless, I had no alternative—I went down the next day and got fitted for uniforms. I shudder to think of how close I came to not getting the job that made such a difference in my life.

It wasn't too long after I joined Duke that we embarked on a southern tour. Among the tobacco barns, skating rinks, cotton warehouses, and fields, there were some theaters. Our reception was tremendous, and we were compelled to do many extra shows. It almost seemed like a continuous performance because we would barely finish a show and take a smoke when Jonesy would be yelling, "All on!"

Everybody started looking shaggy behind the ears, which led to some of the braver lads getting a hair trim from each other.

Wallace Jones, first trumpet man, was perhaps the most skilled among the amateur barbers, but his touch was too vigorous for Duke's tender scalp, so I was elected. After that, whenever we were caught in a situation where haircuts weren't available, I would be pressed into service as Duke's barber.

The fellows spent quite a lot of time making sure that they were well groomed. According to the high standards set by Duke, they could do no less, because only an idiot could have missed being aware of the great effort Ellington made to present perfection in every detail.

A memorable example comes to mind. For the very important Congress Hotel debut in Chicago, the Governor (as the fellows sometimes called Duke) outdid himself, outfitting us in crimson trousers, special-made crimson shoes, which set off the white mess jackets, boiled shirts with winged collars, and white ties. Duke was overheard saying, "They may not like our music, but we sure look pretty." We received an ovation before we played a note. One newspaper critic devoted two-thirds of his column to our appearance and mentioned the incongruity of my battered metal derby. The rest of the brass section had bright and shiny derbies to play their horns into, but not Fat Stuff.

There also was the opening at the Roxy Theater in New York City that was outstanding enough to mention. This was an important date, as we could tell by the way Ellington conferred with so many people. In his dressing room, there were sketches of the stage set. Duke scanned these for days while we were playing the Apollo Theater uptown, and then we were told to go to the tailor for fittings on the new uniforms. Here's what he came up with: cinnamon-brown slacks, chocolate-brown jackets, billiard-green shirts, pastel-yellow ties. Black shoes and socks completed the get-up.

However, at the dress rehearsal at the Roxy, Duke took one look at our color scheme and immediately dashed to the phone and awakened some shirt manufacturer with an order for several dozen shirts of a different color. Then, he explained that the original shirts muddied our features under the lights. But we used them for one-nighters later.

As imaginative as Ellington's conception for the organization was, his personal attire was even more avant garde. I shall never forget one effect created when he stepped onstage wearing a black satin jacket, black satin weskit, black-and-white checkered slacks, a custom-made white shirt with a beautiful collar (self-designed), topped off with a beige cravat, and worn with black suede shoes.

Then there was the unforgettable, show-stopping ensemble he wore at the Downtown Cotton Club once. This had to be seen to be believed. It was on an Easter Sunday, and, as usual, the band played an overture. Then there came a pause as Duke made his dramatic entrance attired in a salmon-colored jacket and fawn-gray slacks and shoes. The shirt, I remember, was a tab-collared oyster shade and his tie some indefinable pastel between salmon and apricot. The audience cheered for at least two minutes.

While Ellington's sartorial qui vive has been duly noted and commented on from time to time, there has been no comment in depth about his profound influence on men's fashions. Duke combines the luxurious aplomb of an Oriental potentate with the considered good taste of a true artist. It is not my intention to imply that our friend invented the wrap-around buttonless top coat, the square-toed soft-leather shoes, the large spread collar that became known as the Barrymore, or the other trends that I saw first as he wore them. But it is safe to say that he did, and does, lead, while others follow. Currently, it's the three-inch cuff on his trousers that will perhaps catch on.

It was long ago when Duke was making *Check and Double Check*, his first movie. En route to California, he met the people who ran a theatrical shoe firm in Chicago. He had them make a dozen pairs of a shoe he designed—feather-weight, thin-soled, square-toed. This evolved, over some twenty or so years, into what is now known as the Italian shoe. But at the time, this way-out footwear was a real conversation piece. Duke continued to order these shoes by the dozen, in every imaginable color and leather, and had soon accumulated so many pairs that he had to have special trunks made to accommodate them.

It was always his custom to change shoes between sets, choosing between the blacks in calf and patent leather, the browns in crocodile, alligator, and suede, and all the other colors in the spectrum. When I attended a few concerts by the band recently, I was amazed that he didn't change shoes. Later I found out the reason. These were the pumps he had worn when he was presented to the Queen of England, and despite their shabby appearance, they now were his favorites.

Another of his idiosyncrasies is his extreme annoyance at losing a button off a garment. I have often seen him abruptly stride off stage to change after a button fell off. During that period when I was with the band, some lucky fellow would be the proud possessor of an Ellington suit or jacket, as Duke would not wear a garment after it lost a button.

In the past, it was always a source of amusement to me when certain newspapers and magazines would publish a list of the best-dressed men of the world. Cary Grant, the Duke of Windsor, etc., would usually lead the polls, but the elegant Ellington never made it, to my knowledge. This unquestionably was a case of being overlooked, or perhaps the arbiters of male styles are not hip enough to be hip to Duke.

While Ellington made no best-dressed lists, the band was winning music polls. Even his most loyal followers couldn't understand how the band could be so great with such seeming lack of discipline. They wondered how all of this inventiveness and beautiful music could be produced as bandsmen drift on and off stage, yawn, act bored, apparently disdaining the people, the music, and the entire scene.

I have seen what appeared to be a re-enactment of rush hour at Grand Central Station or the changing of the guard at Buckingham Palace on Ellington's bandstand. I have been amused, in retrospect, at one of the bandsmen's chewing gum with great vigor, as he read a book while playing his part. That was my contribution to the disorder. Where else but in Ellington's band could that happen? The ground rules, per se, for musicians just do not apply to these special musicians nor to their leader. He chooses people who best portray his music, regardless of their social attitudes or habits.

This all seems indicative of Duke's character or lack of character, but it is only on the surface. Underneath the obvious, there sits this leader, calmly, analytically observing the various personalities of his troops, man by man. His approach differs with each individual. Right on the bandstand, decisions are pondered, punishments meted out, rewards given on the spot. But all that is evident to the audience is vaguely controlled chaos. I have observed with intense curiosity and awe how this master chess player manipulates the musical pawns on his scene.

It has been said that Duke never fires a man. That is substantially correct. However, once he has decided on a change, a change happens. Duke creates a situation that the fellow finds untenable, and he quits. He gets the message.

Despite the glamour of being with the organization and the generally easygoing atmosphere, there was still plenty to grumble about. The constant travel, especially the one-nighters, was a sore spot with a lot of guys. The problem of eating was perhaps the biggest headache. Our fare was usually the quickly snatched, cooked-to-death hamburger or something equally vile from the local greasy spoon.

If we played a theater with enough time between shows, Wellman Braud, the Louisiana bass player, sometimes put on a pot of red beans and rice, smothered pork chops, or some other soul-satisfying dish. The fellows were so delighted that Billy Taylor—the band's other bassist, and I decided to pitch in with the cooking. We bought pots and pans and sterno stoves and cooked up a breeze. I'll never forget the time we put on a big frying pan of onions and garlic just before show time, planning to cook liver as soon as the show was over and have a quick dinner. We gave Jonesy instructions to turn off the onions as soon as they were browned. Halfway through the performance, the faint aroma of fried onions began to waft on stage. I turned around and looked at Braud and Taylor, who both stood playing near Duke. Billy had a sickly grin on his face, and Braud was making violent gestures. It wasn't until after the show that I realized he was trying to signal me to go backstage and take the stuff off the stove. Jonesy had forgot, and the dressing room was full of smoke, while the theater virtually reeked of burned onions. The manager was tearing around backstage red-faced and furious. We never cooked in that theater again.

Besides easing the pangs of hunger, musicians also have a need to ease the tedium of travel and kill time while waiting for the show to go on. On trains, buses, or aboard ship, we Ellingtonians usually had several games of cards going—gin rummy, tonk (a form of rummy), black jack, bridge, red dog, pinochle, and especially stud poker. We favored stud poker over every other game. I held my own as a rule but never cleaned up like Ivie Anderson, the band's singer, or Duke did. They would "win the table" as the boys say, win so much that nobody would want to go on with the game.

My bitter experience came one morning in the middle of the Atlantic. I had won the table and sent almost everyone to his cabin. The game was over with the exception of Duke, who leered at me, sleepy-eyed, across the poker table, saying, "Why don't we have some wine to brighten us up? After all, you won't be able to sleep, winning all of that dough."

I was about $1,500 ahead, so I agreed, feeling invincible. We began toasting each other between bets. That champagne started tasting better and better, and the bets grew bigger and bigger. The next thing I knew, I was in my cabin fully dressed, but I had lost my shirt—I was busted.

Duke is a natural-born winner. He has won every conceivable musical honor, and without question he has earned the tremendous homage that his genius has brought him. He wears his honors lightly and gracefully, never losing sight of his roots and heritage but yet transcending his environmental origins. I have been close enough to and also far enough away from Duke to see the inevitable change in him as a person. His transition from Washington and Room Ten to command performances for royalty was a long and arduous trail, speckled by the various joys and sorrows of life. And even Ellington is not exempt from the immutable law of change. He grows grander but more introspective. He has apparently learned to give more of himself in public but less in private.

The strain of constantly being on stage has taken its toll, the hassels with band personnel, with bookers, with schemers and parasites who attempt to pinch a bit off the top. These all have caused the famed bags under his eyes to grow baggier. The hail fellow, well met, who was a buddy to his boys is no longer there —and understandably so. As he sardonically proclaims "I love you madly" to his admiring followers, I wonder if he has not subconsciously hypnotized himself into really believing it. But I don't need to conjecture about those of us who played in the band he made great—to us he will always be the Boss, and we *do* love him madly.

Sketches in a Ducal Vein

REAMS OF WORDS have been written about Duke Ellington and virtually every aspect of the Ellington mystique has been explored. Many know him to be a creative, talented innovator of popular music and also an uncanny magician who must be unschooled musically by academic standards yet nonetheless manages to confound his critics and delight the public, year after year. Certainly, these are significant aspects of the man. But there's also Ellington the fastidious fop, the daring delineator of sophisticated bons mots designed to dazzle the ladies, and the suave hipster who is equally adept at telling tall tales with the boys on the corner. Unquestionably, under that cool "we love you maadly" facade lies a subterranean welter of controversial character qualities.

Ellington is not a man who can be judged by ordinary yardsticks. As befits any man of genius, we are compelled to utilize an entirely different system of balances and counterbalances. In Ellington's case, his personality covers all of the bases and extensions of human behavior. He is a composite of each character quality and its exact opposite. He is both generous and stingy; thoughtful and inconsiderate; dependable and irresponsible; etc. And etc. While all of us have a smattering of contradictory aspects to our personality, in the Duke these cover the entire spectrum. To be more specific, Duke can be generous to a fault and stingy to an equal fault. He bestowed on his younger sister, Ruth, eighteen years his junior, all the lavish accoutrements of a young princess, as he exemplified the grand Duke. At twelve or thirteen, she had her first fur coat. In quick succession came automobiles, jewelry, luxurious apartments, town houses, and apparel from the best stores in Washington and New York. Yet, money can be a touchy subject. He once allowed one of the stars of the band (Cootie Williams) to leave the organization rather than give him a twenty-five dollar-a-week raise!

Duke's generosity or lack of it does not follow a pattern. He often picks up the tab for a large party, but will cadge cigarettes. While he is inclined to be gracious to his family, his son Mercer was not permitted to play the role of rich man's son. Although Mercer was given the comforts to which he was entitled, when he reached young manhood, he was expected to work, and in this, he was not allowed to follow his own mind. After Mercer won a scholarship in aero engineering at a highly rated institution, Duke vetoed the project and remained adamant, refusing to permit his son to continue these studies. Perhaps Duke had hopes of starting a musical dynasty? Today, Mercer holds down a trumpet chair in the band, never featured nor soloed, his only distinction being that he doubles as band manager. On stage, Duke projects an image of youthful exuberance which would do credit to a far younger man. While leading some of his bouncier tunes, he does a sort of go-go dance, his rhythmic movements cuing the musicians. Yet he can turn about in a flash and be found moaning and groaning on a couch, telephoning his medico and fast friend, Arthur Logan, to rush to his side (perhaps from thousands of miles away). He leans heavily on his supply of vitamins and pills to keep him in good health.

Knowledgeable about food and wines, Duke certainly qualifies as a gourmet. But his concern about his health often keeps him on a grapefruit and steak diet, no matter the type of restaurant or what the choices are. Ellington has a mad passion for rich ice cream and will sometimes ignore his diet when a superb ice cream is available. And of course, the best is always available to Duke Ellington. For many years, restaurants have vied for the honor of catering lavish meals to his dressing room. This was fortunate for him in the days when Negroes were not served in the downtown area of many cities. The bandmen did not fare so well, and Duke was oblivious. Once, it took a full-fledged band mutiny in Saint Louis to force Ellington to arrange for food for the men, when additional shows prevented us from going to the ghetto area for dinner. Yet, Duke was very concerned about most aspects of the band. Our appearance on stage was of primary importance. Thousands of dollars on tailors' fees were spent for uniforms. One memorable time, when we were to play the Roxy Theater in New York and dress rehearsal revealed that none of our five sets of uniform fitted the color scheme of this particular presentation, a rush order provided us with a sixth outfit—at double prices.

Ellington's personal wardrobe also reflects his consummate taste, with handmade square-toed shoes and tailor-made suits which in some cases he has personally designed. An observer will note such recent style innovations as cuffed jacket sleeves or no-pocket jackets. His cuff links are exquisite but no watch adorns his wrist. As for headgear, he leans toward the most inexpensive hats. Usually a two- or three-dollar deal tops his attire. At a record session, one of these bargain toppers will be rakishly tilted over a sweat shirt and baggy pants outfit. Here, the sartorial Ellington is absent and the genius works in comfort. Frequently, Duke is the last to arrive for a record session. The men have long been seated and tuned up, awaiting their leader—and their music. While Ellington has known about the record date for weeks and perhaps months, the music and score are seldom ready. Writing changes continue throughout the session. On the other hand, this haphazard attitude about time is not true for scheduled night club or concert dates. Duke, the instruments, the band, and their uniforms are on the spot promptly, as per contract, through rain, snow, sleepless nights, or what have you.

Usually, Ellington is affable and pleasant to the men. Instead of a brusque-voiced "tune up, fellows," he will request by suggesting archly, "let's see if the piano is in tune." Ordinarily, not a cross word is said to a man who daydreams through a set, failing to play his parts out of laziness, fatigue, or sheer obstinacy. But in spite of his easy going manner, Duke nonetheless manages to be unapproachable. He will be listening intently to a conversation, but if it takes a turn he doesn't like, he either dashes away or can, while remaining in the room, simply turn off. His eyes glaze over, he stares in another direction, and no amount of further talking can involve him at this point. Duke spends most of his time between sets relaxing in his dressing room in a robe, stocking cap on his head, and a towel draped around his neck. Hordes of well-wishers, fans, bookers, and assorted other hangers-on wait outside for a chance to speak to him. Someone is assigned the job of keeping them all out. Yet, almost as if he had X-ray eyes, Duke knows who is there and with whom.

Nothing, no matter how trivial, escapes his attention, and anything he wants to remember remains in his memory forever. He can recall snatches of tunes, the most obscure person met twenty years before, bits of gossip. But he forgets (or feigns forgetfulness) on many occasions—money he owes, someone he was supposed to phone, or who wrote a tune. There have been instances of his name turning up as co-composer on songs that others thought they wrote. This happened to me on some I recorded (whether or not he had played on the date). But, again, in many instances, it was his approach and arrangements which made the melodies palatable to the public. And Duke got shafted, too—his *Happy-Go-Lucky Local* later came into prominence as *Night Train*, with the composer credits given to someone else.

Of late, Ellington's religious side has come into public view, with the well-publicized presentations of his jazz in and for the church. As he says, we each worship in our own way. Duke has always worn a religious medal and read his bible daily. Yet, I doubt that he has attended services a dozen times in the last few decades. Furthermore, for a religious man he has a large number of superstitions. A strange one concerns loose buttons on his clothing. If a button is hanging by a thread or—even worse—has fallen off, that garment will never be worn by the Duke again. It is up for grabs among the fellows in the band. Here, Ellington displays his generosity to a bandsman who is in favor. Some of the men in his good graces who have coveted a beautiful top coat or sports jacket have been known to deliberately twist a button loose.

There is no doubt that Ellington has enormous charm. Many of the lovely ladies upon whom Duke has cast an approving eye, and then heaped exquisite compliments have succumbed. The number of his conquests is uncountable. Yet, there has always been one in the background to whom he has given special allegiance, contrasting with the short-term dalliances. Ellington is a highly original man in almost every aspect of his personality—his clothes, his music, and his speech quickly display this originality. But once he's created something, he makes it a part of himself and repeats it over and over. He steals from his own tunes and thus gets stuck with cliché patterns. In almost any concert, there is "The Medley" of his hit tunes. Even his biggest fans feel like leaving when this old chestnut offering starts out with the same old fanfare, now some twenty-five years old.

Then, there are the pat phrases, unconvincingly told to all the women. "My, but you make that dress look lovely!" is one of his favorites, along with a few modifications such as "you've made this a beautiful evening." Once, an audience must have given appreciative applause when he flashed his teeth and said, "we love you maadly." Now, it's a part of every program, told not once but perhaps five or six times during the course of a concert. Still, the day doesn't pass when Duke doesn't utter one original bon mot. Unfortunately, if it meets with great response, it may become part of the verbal repertoire.

Duke recently celebrated his sixty-eighth birthday, having enjoyed four decades of great success. He's been presented to royalty, played the world's most famous concert halls, had a postage stamp printed in his honor, written dozens of popular songs, and has influenced countless musicians, song writers, and arrangers. A profile in the *New Yorker*, articles in magazines, newspapers, and even whole books have been devoted to the subject of Duke Ellington. Yet, to this day, no one can draw an accurate thumbnail sketch of his personality. A further exploration of the varied facets of this extraordinary man only confirms the contradictory aspects of his character. The multi-colored spectrum of the paradoxical Duke Ellington adds up to the conclusion that he is a true enigma.

Music Maker, August, 1967

Duke Ellington: One of a Kind

DUKE ELLINGTON is securely famous in his own lifetime, something which rarely happens to a man, especially in music. Still, the journey to the Olympian heights has not been easy for Ellington. He has had to contend with all of the evils of nonrecognition due to the color of his skin, the attendant friction that followed when he dared to be different in his music, plus the personal involvement with life itself, from which no one may escape.

But here is the man who has surmounted the obstacles. He is the first, and perhaps last, of the genuine creative founding fathers of music Americana. This amazing man possesses a sincere dedication to his art, a singleness of purpose toward his high goals, and, fortunately, a great physical stamina which has enabled him to carry on despite the wear and tear on his body. These attributes, however, are not by any means the sum total of Ellington. There's also the imaginative aspect, which for want of a better description I call "knowledgeable derring-do" that lets Duke retain his unique, infectious approach to music in a spirit of adventure, always tasteful and fresh.

The Duke's creativity works in mysterious ways, its wonders to perform. He snatches ideas out of the thin air. Many's the time that I've seen him on the Ellington orchestra's Pullman with his feet propped up and a towel draped over his eyes, seemingly in complete repose. Then, he'd suddenly jump up as if a bee had stung him, grab a scrap of manuscript paper, a yellow pencil, and scribble madly for hours—or sometimes only for a minute. Other times, he has been observed riding in a bus of ancient vintage that seemingly had never heard of springs, jounced around like a dodg'em at a carnival. But the Governor wrote on and on, not concerned as we, the members of his band, were with the lack of comfort. As I recall, it was a rare day that Duke didn't write something, even if it was only four bars.

Ellington was careful to make certain that no one possessed any parts of his music until he chose so, nor did he permit others access to perform it. I recall only two exceptions that he made— when Charlie Barnet's music was destroyed in the fire at the Palomar, Ellington came to his rescue with the loan of arrangements. Later, he helped sponsor Boyd Rayburn's band with both arrangements and money. His normal procedure was to be very cautious. I was utterly fascinated when I first saw him deliberately tear into tiny pieces some music that he had spent hours writing. Then, he flushed it down a toilet drain. I couldn't contain my curiosity, so I asked him why he had destroyed it. His reply stunned me; he answered with a smile, "Well, I'll tell you, Fat Stuff. If it's good, I'll remember it. If it's bad, well I want to forget it and I would prefer that no one catches on to how lousy I can write." During the years that I spent with Duke, this scene was often repeated, and what he said would come back to me as I watched him flush dreams down the drain.

Duke's writing was actually only the frosting on the cake of his genius, as a considerable part of his outpourings stemmed from the entwining of the written projections and the intuitive interpolations by the Ellington orchestra. The final result emerged as a delightful cohesive unity, broad in scope and refreshingly imaginative in its delineation. Duke always refers to the band as his instrument, and he has certainly selected some fine musicians to make up that instrument. With a wealth of talent available, he always chooses musicians whose basic concept is compatible to his way of thinking, and then proceeds to mold them into the organization. Occasionally, others are baffled by his choice of an instrumentalist, but eventually it becomes clear why the man was chosen.

Over the years, the band has been virtually an all-star aggregation, and at present boasts a saxophone section with Paul Gonsalvez, Russell Procope, Jimmy Hamilton, Harry Carney, and the great Johnny Hodges, each a superb player. The brass section has been rejuvenated with the return of Cootie Williams to add to the luster of the phenomenal high-note William "Cat" Anderson. The mainstay is Lawrence Brown on trombone, and recently Duke has been assisted by his son, Mercer, in the trumpet section.

The music they produce seldom seems to have entailed a lot of work, but what the adoring public never realizes and could not know is that in the Ellington organization, there is the combined knowledge of these gifted artists, who by virtue of years of experience are able to create, on the spot, any mood that they choose. And with this array of talent, it is small wonder that Duke maintains his position of preeminence.

Part of Ellington's international recognition stems from his very successful records. These have been created in a completely unorthodox manner. The usual procedure, in the business of making records, with such bands as Count Basie's or Woody Herman's, say, is to rely for the most part on a written score, with the various parts assigned to the respective instruments on separate sheets of paper. However, Duke confounds his contemporaries with his departures from this procedure. Half of the time, there'll be no written parts, and on arriving at the studio, everybody will sit around smoking, noodling on their horns, and reading while waiting for Ellington. He usually dashes in fifteen minutes late (and, on reflection, I speculate that we were always called early to allow for any late-comers). In any case, Duke makes his entrance trailed by his alter ego and sometime collaborator, Billy "Sweetpea" Strayhorn, or Tom Whaley, who has the unenviable role of music copyist for Ellington. Duke's writing is of a special personal quality, and his musical shorthand has baffled many a copyist, but Whaley, a competent arranger in his own right (although Ellington has never utilized this skill), seems to have a sixth sense concerning what Duke has in mind when he comes on with those peculiar musical hieroglyphics.

After saying hello to any guy who catches his eye, Duke seats himself at the piano and will either rhapsodize lazily, with his thoughts way up in the clouds, or he may break into a fast stomp reminiscent of a cutting session thirty-five years ago at True Reformers Hall in Washington, D.C. This is what he calls his warm-up, and we would know that the first number was to be something swinging, perhaps the still unintelligible tune that he hummed so loudly. Once that is over, the next thing we might hear is Duke saying, "All right, fellows, let's see if the piano is in tune." That means everybody tune up, which was the first thing we'd done on arrival, but he has to hear the sound from the various instruments.

Then, the fun begins as Duke reaches into his pocket, and with the air of a magician produces some scraggly pieces of manuscript paper—about one-eighth of a page on which he'd scribbled some notes. I recall one occasion when he'd jotted some notes for the saxophones (Toby Hardwick, Harry Carney, Ben Webster, and Barney Bigard) and each was given a part, but there was nothing for Johnny Hodges. Duke had the saxes run the sequence down twice, while Johnny sat nonchalantly smoking. Then, Duke called to Hodges, "Hey, Rabbit, give me a long slow glissando against that progression. Yeah! That's it!" Next he said to Cootie Williams, "Hey, Coots, you come in on the second bar, in a subtle manner growling softly like a hungry little lion cub that wants his dinner but can't find his mother. Try that, okay?" Following that, he'd say, "Deacon," (how Lawrence Brown hated that nickname) "you are cast in the role of the sun beating down on the scene. What kind of a sound do you feel that could be? You don't know? Well, try a high B-flat in a felt hat, play it legato and sustain it for eight bars. Come on, let's all hit this together," and that's the way things went—sometimes.

Then, there'd be times when Strayhorn would precede Ellington into the studio and take over the rehearsal perhaps for an hour when we'd get every nuance down to perfection, but you could bet when Duke arrived there'd be some changes made. He'd have us run it down again, while he listened with a critical ear. Then, he'd call for changes, perhaps starting with bar sixteen, playing eight bars, then back to letter C and when we got to letter E, he'd call a halt. Then, he'd sit at the piano and play something, have a consultation with Tom Whaley, and some new music would be scored on the spot.

Sometimes, this "new" music would be a creative lick that one of the musicians had played at a dance months before, proving that Duke was never too involved to hear what was going on in the band—and also displaying his fantastic memory. More than once, a lick which started out as a rhythmic background for a solo or a response to another lick, eventually became a hit record, once Duke's fertile imagination took over and provided the proper framework.

Among Ellington's lesser known talents is that of lyric writing. To me, the best example of his work is the words to *The Blues* which was a part of his suite *Black, Brown, and Beige*. As I remember, the words begin:

> *The blues*
> *The blues ain't*
> *The blues ain't nothin' but a cold grey day*
> *And all night long, they stay that way.*

This lyric is a warm extension of another facet that dwells within the Duke. His words to the ancient *I've Got to be a Rug Cutter* also gassed me, maybe because Ivie Anderson sang them so spiritedly along with the trio from the band composed of Hayes Alvis, Harry Carney, and myself.

Ellington's imagination in giving titles to his music also reflects his poetic bent. He ran through all the shades of blue—*Mood Indigo, Azure, Turquoise Cloud, Transbluecency,* and *Blue Serge.* Some of his more colorful titles were *Pretty and the Wolf, Gal from Joe's, Sophisticated Lady, Frantic Phantasy*—the list goes on and on. The inspiration for these titles came in many ways. Once, we were riding a train to California and entered a succession of undulating, gently molded hills. When we reached a certain place, Duke remarked, "Look at that! Why, that's a perfect replica of a female reclining in complete relaxation, so unashamedly exposing her warm valley." And so a title was born, and shortly thereafter, we recorded *Warm Valley.*

With both words and music, Duke always comes up with something worthwhile. One of the regrets of his life (and I join him in it) is that Broadway never got to see his witty, gay, and inspired musical *Jump for Joy.* This musical was good enough to run for months in Los Angeles, a town that is not noted as a good show town. And, at this point, despite several efforts in the direction of an Ellington Broadway musical, the planets have never been in proper conjunction, and nothing of value has come forth. But here and now I make this prediction, that the day shall come when Edward Kennedy Ellington will dazzle Broadway and the world with a production that people won't be able to forget for a long time.

In Ellington, the facets of personality emerge stronger than they do in the majority of men. As with any public figure, there is great curiosity about the man, and when I am asked about him, I can only answer the question with a question, "Which aspects of Ellington's character are you interested in hearing about?" The man is such a completely original person that almost any aspect of his personality is noteworthy. For example, there's the side of him interested in clothes. He will purchase twenty suits at a time, designed and made to his specifications, or ten pairs of handmade shoes, or three dozen custom-made shirts. And if a button should fall off a jacket, that garment is discarded. Ellington has a superstition about wearing clothes that have lost their buttons. But despite this ostentation, suggesting that of an oriental potentate, he refuses to wear a watch or ring! Another facet is his great sense of loyalty. Once he has established a close relationship, it takes a near cataclysm to break it. For example, the musicians who started with him in his original band remained with him for years, despite the fact that they took advantage of their relationship to the detriment of the band. He dislikes change so much that even when an individual has clearly demonstrated that his personal habits are in conflict with good band morale, it is hard for the Duke to fire him. Those who have conformed apparently have a lifetime job. Harry Carney, for example, has been with Duke for about forty years.

Duke, more than most people, avoids emotional scenes. When some of the aforementioned musicians had brought Duke to a point where most leaders would have fired them, he has instead created a situation sufficiently uncomfortable for them so that they get the message and quit.

With anyone at all, Ellington may terminate a conversation by simply withdrawing his interest. In the beginning, he is charming, affable, and involved in the subject. But once he has, in his mind, exhausted the subject or the person, he starts looking around as if he is seeking escape. Escape he does in a variety of ways. He either answers in disinterested monosyllables, starts a conversation with someone else, or mumbles an excuse and dashes off.

Then, there is Duke the perennial ladies' man. He has certain favorite greetings: "My, you make that dress look lovely." Or, "You're looking more beautiful than ever." Or, "Now I know why I was born—to meet you, my dear." He flashes his devilish smile, and lately has taken to bussing everyone, men included, in the French manner, on each cheek.

But all of that is on the superficial level. Personally, Edward Kennedy Ellington remains an enigma to most people, and that includes me. Duke is not a man who blows hot and cold—there's always a warm greeting for everyone, with few exceptions. He is solicitous, always asks about one's family along with other small talk of common interest, but the better you know him, the more you realize that you don't really know him at all. He is the iceberg—only the small, flamboyant portion that he wishes to display is visible, and the large part is hidden away from all but a very select few.

Although I departed from the band exactly twenty years ago, I still find my regard for him and the organization undiminished, so I always make it my business to visit with them whenever they are not too far away. A few years ago, the band played a dance in Los Angeles. I went. After chatting with some of my old buddies in the band, I knocked on the Governor's door. (I usually called him Governor, but had other, not so polite, nicknames, such as Dumpy.) I was answered by a grunt which could have been interpreted as either "come in" or "stay out." I entered anyway, immediately perceiving the familiar sight of Duke stretched full-length on a couch in a dressing gown, with the usual towel over his eyes, and greeted him by saying, "Mr. Ellington, I believe?" He replied, without raising his head, "Why Fat Stuff! How nice of you to drop by! How's the family?" After a few such remarks, we both became silent, and I got ready to leave; I felt that the moment of rapport was over. Then, he startled me by saying, "You know, you should sue so-and-so for taking your tune." He was referring to a melody which I had recorded on one of the Ellington small band dates many years before. It was later re-titled and recorded by someone else, and became a standard, with no credits going to me. Knowing that Duke was putting me on, I replied, "That's right, and I wonder when you are going to sue what's-his-name. After all, he took your *Happy-Go-Lucky Local* note for note!" This evoked a big laugh from the Governor, and we parted with him saying, "I want to see you before we leave. There's something that I want to talk to you about." Later, during the evening, he told Harry Carney to remind me that he wanted me to see him before he left, but because of the press of fans and well-wishers, I never did get close enough to him to find out what we were to discuss.

About a year later, he telephoned me around 3:00 A.M., saying in typical Ellington fashion, "Hey, Fat Stuff, how much longer do you intend to be on your vacation from the band?" It turned out that after the twenty-year absence, he wanted me to make a European tour with the band. I was indeed flattered, but reluctantly had to tell the Governor that I couldn't make it on such short notice because of my other commitments.

Ellington is far more of a hero in Europe than he is in his own country. I shall never forget hearing 5,000 school children serenade him in Sweden on his birthday. And Ellington's audiences, from the international standpoint, are steadily becoming greater, due to his more frequent overseas tours. He prefers to have his contributions known as American Negro music rather than jazz. Paradoxically, the American Negro by and large couldn't care less about Ellington's music, and considers it old hat and not in his groove. And in the commercial atmosphere which permeates this country, whatever Ellington projects musically is always labeled "jazz," much to the Duke's dismay.

However, Duke has no intention of permitting his personal feelings to interfere with getting his Negro music across to a dwindling American public. Very seldom can you turn on a radio nowadays and hear Ellington. Juke boxes rarely have even one Ellington record. Fortunately, television in the last few years has belatedly started to recognize his efforts.

Ellington, the creative piano-playing leader of one of the most consistent evolutionary forces in American popular music, has not only enriched the music, he has also had a tremendous influence on musicians. Those of us who have had the privilege of working with Duke are constantly reminded of the debt that we owe him for being allowed to be in his orbit. Time has brought into being a camaraderie among those of us who consider ourselves his disciples. Hopefully, what we have learned about life and music under the aegis of the boss will be spread and will continue as a permanent force in American popular music. Even as we think these thoughts, we are fully aware that we can never measure up to the stature of this giant, for he is Duke Ellington, one of a kind.

Evergreen Review, December, 1966

Tribute to Tricky Sam (Joe Nanton)

OVER THE YEARS, many musicians have been capable, many ordinary. Some display talent momentarily and then fade into oblivion. Only a few have had that something, that rare gift of communication that Joseph Nanton had.

Better known as Tricky Sam, Nanton was one of the most important voices in Duke Ellington's orchestra, and during his tenure (1926 to 1948) he became internationally famous. The nickname Tricky Sam was probably coined by the ubiquitous Otto Hardwick, since Toby (as the musicians of Harlem nicknamed the elegant Washingtonian) enjoyed giving musicos noms de plume that fitted their personalities. In this instance, no better sobriquet could have been found, because Nanton was a complex man. On the surface, he was mild-mannered. Before the public he was at various times a clown, a tragedian, or merely the fellow on the corner, depending on the role that Duke had assigned him.

Joseph Nanton in private was a scholar, a fierce nationalist and devoted follower of Marcus Garvey back in the thirties (when political awareness was unheard of from a musician). However, this thinking, knowledgeable man kept his lives separate, and only a few of his chums were ever aware of his inner thoughts. But the external facade he presented was always warm and friendly.

Ellington's Joe Nanton was a gingerbread-colored man, kind of on the squatty side. His facial contours reminded me of a benevolent basset hound, with those big brown eyes that regarded the world so dolefully, framed in a long face with just a hint of dewlaps.

Of much more importance are the motivations, the strengths, weaknesses, and all the other facets that comprised this extraordinary individual.

Nanton's playing differed from that of virtually all other trombonists in jazz. His sound was a voice unique to the instrument, and although many of his fellows played sweeter, faster, louder, and with considerably more technique, still Tricky possessed the gift of communication that is the essence of any music. Others have tried to copy his plunger style, including Al Grey, Tricky Lofton, Quentin Jackson, and even the impeccable Lawrence Brown, but none has been able to capture his sound and nuance. They were all mere echoes of Tricky.

What a variety of sounds he evoked from his instrument! From the wail of a new-born baby to the raucous hoot of an owl, from the bloodcurdling scream of an enraged tiger to the eerie cooing of a mourning dove, Tricky had them all in his bag of tricks, and he utilized them with thoughtful discretion and good taste. He was a natural musician, gifted with that extra something that cannot be taught by teachers, although he credited two fellows with forming his style, Charlie Irvis, who preceded him with Ellington, and Jake Green of Charleston, South Carolina, whom we called Gutbucket.

The New York cabarets were jumping back in the days when Joe Nanton appeared on the Turf, the center of which was 135th Street from Fifth Avenue to Lenox Avenue. There were a lot of clubs in the area—there was O'Connor's on the uptown side of the street and the Green Parrot upstairs over the Gem Theater. Tricky once worked at the Green Parrot but later remarked that he quit because he got tired of going to jail every Saturday night. On the corner of Fifth Avenue was Leroy's Club, which was considered a big-time spot, since Leroy was the brother of Baron Wilkins (at that time, the boss of Harlem). Wilkins' 134th Street club catered strictly to the underworld, and this is the place where I first saw Tricky. He was working there with piano man Fat Smitty and a hell of a drummer, known simply as Crip.

Down Fifth Avenue a few doors, across 135th Street, Edwin Smalls operated his first club, the Sugar Cane. Then, farther down, between 132nd and 133rd, as I recall, was a joint run by a fellow named Edmonds, whose claim to fame is that Ethel Waters sang there. This was also the place where I first got acquainted with Nanton, around 1923.

The group consisted of Tricky, pianist Earl Frazier, Crip again on drums, and Seminole the Indian on banjo (who later became better known as a piano man). Nanton was then fresh out of San Juan Hill and about eighteen years old. He had an indefinable quality about him even then that made him ageless. Perhaps it was his high, squeaky voice, which sometimes would fade away to a mere whisper. Or maybe it was his general air of insouciance. When we got to hanging around together, I knew Joe as a Charleston-dancing, uke-playing funster.

During the twenties, musicians had it so good that you could get fired at 11 P.M. and by midnight be sitting on another band-stand blowing for the tips. The kitty was soon full of folding money, which visiting musicians shared in as well as the regulars, as long as the visitors were well liked and could blow. Tricky, being well liked, was all over Harlem. Of course, some clubs had better-spending patrons, and some drew bigger crowds. Consequently, the guys battled for those choice spots. A job at Edmond's club was one of the most sought after, since the place catered to ladies of the evening, who were notorious for drowning their sorrows and throwing money away.

But everyone moved around a lot, since a few weeks or months was long enough to stay in one spot, and, too, the fellows would move about on account of their teammate. In those days, a pair of brass men (trumpets and trombones) usually hung out as a team, eating and drinking and especially playing together. There were Bubber Miley and Charlie Irvis, Geechy Fields and Gus Aikens, Jimmy Harrison and June Clark. My partner was a New Jersey trombonist named Herb Gregory. Tricky's trumpet buddy was Louis Metcalf.

Tricky Sam was always the life of any party, a great trencherman who could put away two or three orders of corned beef hash at Tabb's famed hash house. And when the cats gathered at a cabaret like the Bucket of Blood or Goldgrabbens to jam and talk, Tricky's high-pitched voice could be heard above everybody else's. Before he got the name Tricky Sam, Joe was some times called the Professor, because he knew something about almost everything.

I can see him now, tuxedo crumpled, board-stiff tux shirt speckled with stains of "top 'n bottom" (a lethal mixture of gin and port wine that we drank only in Harlem).

We had a curious way of choosing friends in that era. It depended on how well the man played and how free he was with his money (it was the custom for everyone to buy everybody drinks). And, to be considered a regular cat, a fellow had to hit the Turf (that meant anywhere in the vicinity of the Rhythm Club) immaculate, in a clean, boiled tux shirt between six and ten P.M. After midnight, however, if a guy showed up without "top 'n bottom" stains on his shirt, the gang would drift away sneering that he was not fit to drink with. During those days, it was a rare and square tooter who hit the sack before the sun was high in the sky.

After those frequent nights on the town, Tricky noticed that no matter how much money he had had on him when he and his buddy, Charlie Irvis, started drinking, the next morning he woke up with empty pockets. Not wanting to accuse his buddy, Tricky decided to play detective. He filled a whiskey bottle with tea and proceeded to put on a very convincing drunk act. The pair started home, Charlie high as a kite and Nanton cold sober. When the bar-hopping got hot and heavy, after several stops at various joints, Tricky poured tea into his whiskey glass for the umpteenth time. Then, he heard Irvis say to the bartender, "Rack 'em back, give every tub a taste on me, 'cause me and my buddy got nothin' but money," as he attempted to reach into Tricky's pocket for his wallet. Tricky, sober as a judge, wheezed out in his falsetto voice, "Ya g.d. right, Charlie! Give everybody a drink! And, bartender, give everybody a check or else give their checks to Charlie, because this has been going on long enough. I'm cutting out. So long, Charlie."

All the cats in the bar laughed until they cried as Charlie, shocked to his toes, quickly sobered up and slunk out the door. He called to the retreating Tricky, "Hey, man, wait for me! That ain't no way to treat a buddy." But Tricky was hotfooting it down Seventh Avenue, having learned how his money disappeared.

Starting with this episode, we all noticed a change in Nanton. He stopped being a bar buddy. He kept a bottle in his trombone case, and when he'd go to a joint after working hours, he'd sit at a table and order a setup of glasses and ice. He also switched from "top 'n bottom" to bourbon. Though the feud between him and Irvis did not last long, the relationship was never really the same.

Tricky began holding court at his special table, and almost any morning there'd be at least a dozen fellows sitting around discussing, gossiping, and sometimes heatedly arguing, about anything under the sun.

This was during the period that Joe was playing at the Nest Club in Harlem with Cliff Jackson's Westerners. That was Elmer Snowden's second band, which had replaced us (the first band) while we were at the Bamville Club. And it also was at this time when I really began to develop an insight into Joe Nanton's vast store of knowledge. To my amazement, I discovered what a brain the man possessed. He was well acquainted with such erudite and diverse subjects as astronomy, how to make home brew, and how to use a slide rule. He could recite poetry by ancient poets that most of us never knew existed, and he knew Shakespeare.

In a sense, the Nanton changeover was good for all of us, because it made us think in new directions, and for Tricky too, since he had to stay sober enough to cast his pearls before his audience.

There was one time when I had been put out of my rooming house for being unruly. Russell Procope, my old buddy, came to my rescue with a bed for a few days in his place, which was just down the street from where Tricky lived with his family on 137th Street. One morning, Joe, Russell, and I were meandering home, when on turning the corner, we saw fire engines in the middle of the block. Procope noticed them first and gasped, "Oh my God, my house is on fire!" It turned out to be Tricky's place instead. Smoke was billowing from the windows of the floor above Nanton's apartment, and firemen were evacuating people from the building. Tricky took a startled look at this sight and rushed for the front door. The firemen tried to stop him, but he pushed them aside. In no time at all, he emerged triumphantly, clutching a paper bag to his chest. He explained that his money had been hidden under the livingroom rug. We didn't believe him until he opened the bag and showed us gobs of fifty-dollar bills among the twenties and tens. He must have had a thousand dollars in that stash.

When Joe Nanton replaced his old buddy, Charlie Irvis, in the Ellington band, he played his trombone parts capably and eagerly waited, night after night, for Duke to let him take his "Boston," what the cats called soloing in those days. This went on for weeks as the newcomer literally sat on the edge of his seat waiting to show what he could do, but Duke never gave him the nod, doubtless because the arrangements were mostly built around Bubber Miley and Toby at that time. Duke seemingly remained oblivious until Otto Hardwick, Duke's hometown crony and first sax man, yelled, "For Christ's sake, Dumpy, how long are you gonna let this man sit here without taking a Boston?"

Duke, with that famous sheepish grin, said, "Oh, yes. I've been saving him for the big punch. Sure, take it, Tricky."

One of Tricky's most admirable attributes was his loyalty to Ellington, and this extreme devotion is so rare that it is worthy of mention. Often in the profession, a bunch of fellows will get together and like what they produce so much that it takes a lot of adverse circumstance to pry them apart. However, nine times out of ten, the inevitable breaking up of the group happens—it's one of the hazards of the game.

In the case of Tricky Sam, it's possible that some reader may comment, "Big deal—so he stayed with Duke for twenty-two years. Why wouldn't he stay with one of the better bands, with a steady paycheck coming in all of that time?" The truth of the matter is (and probably not many people remember) that there was a time around 1926, when Tricky joined Ellington, that there were plenty of lean weeks. Any job could well turn out to be of short duration, and back in those days, any road trip might wind up in Strandsville. Tricky was a tower of strength, whether times were good or bad. Duke could always count on him to make the job, and not only that—Joe was so loyal that he refused to work for anyone else, not even a casual club date or a recording session. I consider myself fortunate to have had him on one of my small-band Ellington dates.

To the fellows in the band, an unforgettable sequence will always be remembered as an example of Nanton's savoir-faire put to an exacting test.

The setting was New York City's Grand Central Station, and the audience was a large contingent of priests and nuns congregated in front of the gate where the Ellington party was scheduled to depart for Chicago. I gathered that some dignitary of the church was leaving on the same train, and the throng was there to see him off.

Meanwhile, we Ellingtonians grew saltier and saltier by the minute as we waited for the last member of our troupe. An officious gateman refused to let us board until we were all present and accounted for. The departure time drew closer and closer— still no Nanton. Finally, just when it began to look as if Grand Central Station and Mr. Duke Ellington were going to have a falling-out, there appeared a swirl of motion at the far edge of the crowd. Tricky dashed into view, and we all felt like cheering, until the moment he burst through the crowd. Suddenly, there was an unmistakable crash. The familiar scent of good bourbon pervaded the air. We looked at each other with the same thought: "Oh my God, Tricky's dropped his bottle—and among all of these religious people." That's where Joseph Nanton proved himself. He greeted Ellington without breaking stride or looking at all discomfited: "Greetings, Governor. I thought that I was not going to make it. Sorry, old chap."

On occasion, Nanton could be very British. He wore Brooks Brothers clothes, English handmade shoes, and generally attired himself like a British gentleman. But despite the elegance of his wardrobe and care of grooming, his appearance never transcended that of the man in the street. He always reminded me of Charlie Chaplin. There was a similarity in spirit—they both projected the image of a born loser. Tricky's sad-looking face shows how much appearances can deceive, since sadness could not have been further from the fact. He was a fun lover from 'way back, a practical joker, a convivial drinker.

Born in 1904, Joseph was the middle of three sons of the West Indian Nanton family. He was proud of being West Indian and was brought up in San Juan Hill, one of the scattered colored ghettos of New York City. The Hill area consisted of six square blocks bounded by Ninety-seventh Street and 103rd Street.

Tricky once confided to me that he felt fortunate in having been born in New York City, where the educational advantages for Negroes far surpassed those of most other cities, particularly those below the Mason-Dixon line. Moreover, he was convinced that the West Indians particularly appreciated and took advantage of the opportunities that the North offered them. This brought on a heated discussion, until he quoted statistics (which he documented with printed material) showing how many different businesses the West Indians owned and operated.

Nanton had no patience with ignorance and, commenting on the stupidity of the bulk of the masses, used to say, "Look at them! Head buried in that newspaper, and if you ask them what they are reading, the only thing they can tell you is the baseball scores or about Little Orphan Annie."

To me, this smacked of snobbism, West Indian style, until I

questioned him and was amazed at his depth. He owned hundreds of books on the most erudite subjects, ranging from psychology to philosophy, from history to astronomy.

Joe Nanton usually acted calm, cool, and collected and almost always gave the other fellow the benefit of the doubt. But when someone tried to take advantage of him or his friends, Tricky would stand up for what he believed to be right.

The last time I observed Tricky in this role, the Ellingtonians were doing a tour of Texas. Among the dates there was a peculiar one-nighter scheduled for the Fourth of July in a remote section. Everyone felt a bit nervous because this burg was way off the beaten track, and I guess we subconsciously expected to see Indians jump out from the bushes, shooting arrows at our special train, which was only a Pullman, baggage car, and an engine. After miles of sagebrush, jack rabbits, and nothingness, not seeing even a single Indian, we finally arrived. By that, I mean that the train stopped at a water tower, and we piled into several vehicles that took us over the prairie. I remember Barney Bigard's saying, "Hmm, this sure is a nice section for a necktie party." The remark was not amusing at the time.

In any case, smack in the middle of all that nothingness stood a dance hall. We played harder than usual, not wanting to rile these people who had come in droves (from Lord knows where). They liked what we played until we played *Home Sweet Home* and started packing up. Then the cheers turned to jeers, and we hastily put our horns away and headed for the door. A giant of a fellow leaped onto the bandstand, grabbed the microphone, and said:

"Ladies and gentlemen, this heah dance was advertised as a dawn dance. Now I know that I am full of red eye, jes' lak evahbody else heah, but ah don' see nairy dawn breakin' no wheah, an ah 'spect to heah this music goin' till dawn. Right?"

Rebel yells and Indian war whoops greeted this speech, and for the moment it looked as if our time had come, way out there in the lone prairie.

We were thunderstruck, not knowing if this character was serious or not, but we were resigned to doing whatever we had to, even if it meant unpacking and playing more hours.

Duke appeared cool, although I heard him whisper to the band manager, "Go get the sheriff. Go get the sheriff, for Christ's sake." Ellington was smiling when he said it, but we could tell he was anxious too.

The band manager, who happened to be a Texan himself, answered, "Get the sheriff? Hell, that's the sheriff talking!"

The situation was tense, but Tricky broke the spell when he told a young fellow who tried to grab his horn:

"Watch out, cowboy, that's my living you're fooling with. Mess with it, and you're messing with me."

He looked up at the gangling youngster, at least a head taller, and his attitude indicated that he really wasn't afraid. Then Tricky calmly strutted out of the door while the crowd roared with laughter, and we all filed out after him. We marveled at the kind of strength that, under pressure, could transform a meek little man, a Negro from New York City, into a Napoleon who could intimidate a Texan in Texas.

Life in a touring organization is a constant succession of trains and buses and thus leaves everyone with much boring time to fill. In most bands, the fellows play cards to help pass the hours. Ellington's group was no exception, and we played lots of tonk (a fast form of gin rummy), poker, and on rare occasions, if Ellington was not around, there would be a crap game. One way or another, lots of money changed hands. Everybody played except Tricky. We would find him in a corner reading some tome.

One night while we were playing a theater engagement, the dancers started up a crap game. First Sonny Greer tried his luck, and, one by one, we all became involved. Tricky read on until, in desperation over losing so much money, Sonny called to him, "Come on, Tricky. Roll 'em for me. Maybe you can change the luck for me—I can't do anything right." Tricky demurred but finally was persuaded. He made eight or nine straight passes, to Sonny's delight. Tricky broke everybody and, to my knowledge, never shot craps again.

Joe Nanton never was a person who cared for pomp. He was

not born that way, and when he died in a San Francisco hotel in 1948, he did so in the manner that he had lived—unpretentiously. One afternoon the band bus was scheduled to leave. Although the band waited and waited, this time Tricky did not show. Finally, Lawrence Brown, who had the room next to Tricky's, went to see what was keeping his section mate. Getting a pass key and entering the room, he saw that Joseph Nanton was dead. Thus was silenced one of the most original voices ever heard in the vocabulary of jazz sounds.

Down Beat, January 26, 1967

Illustrious Barney Bigard

ALBANY LEON BIGARD is one of the illustrious sons of New Orleans. He is also one of the clarinetists taught by the Tio family, Papa Tio and his nephew, Lorenzo. Evidently, there was unusual rapport between this musical Mexican clan and fledgling clarinetists, for the Tios sent out an impressive list of artists to dazzle the worlds of jazz and classical music.

Among the Tio jazz scholars were Albert Nicholas, Jimmie Noone, Omer Simeon, and, of course, Barney Bigard. But in the beginning, Bigard's tone on the clarinet was not something of which the Tios would have approved. It was quite a while after Bigard started playing that he became accepted as a professional by fellow musicians.

Barney describes his tone then as something horrible, resulting in his being nicknamed the Snake Charmer. Barney enjoyed the nickname at first, feeling he was now one of the gang. Then one night he overheard a drummer (who later became big in the business) tell a friend: "Guess who's on clarinet tonight—that g.d. Snake Charmer!" The remark made him feel like going through the pavement, Barney says. It also had a positive effect—Bigard decided that he was going to become one of the best clarinet players that New Orleans had ever known. He started woodshedding at home, in addition to taking lessons from Lorenzo Tio.

With one of those hearty bursts of laughter for which he is known, Bigard relived the scene of his brothers, Alexander and Sidney, going through the house with their fingers in their ears. And even Papa Bigard, who was a music lover, found things to do outside the house when Barney started practicing.

Barney was about twelve when Johnny Dodds (who played in the band of Emile Bigard, Barney's uncle) lent him an E-flat clarinet, an instrument chosen because Barney's small fingers could not cover the wider key span on a B-flat clarinet.

It wasn't too long before the men who had put him down began competing with each other for his services. In those days, as Barney tells it, every musician had a little book in which to write down data concerning his dates—time, place, pay. The money was of paramount importance; it would run from seventy-five cents to $1.50 for a dance or funeral. All the musicians would accept several gigs for the same night and then, at the last minute, choose the one that suited them the most, judging this either by the pay or by whom they would be playing with. Thus the ex-Snake Charmer was in a position to snub some of the cats who formerly had derided him.

Bigard is a fine fusion of French, Spanish, Indian, and Negro, with a coloration that is almost white. He is Creole, of an imposing, dignified appearance that belies his occupation. His patrician profile is a facsimile of an old Roman's, with prominent nose, deep-set eyes, and an expression of benign tolerance. Barney is the second of three sons born to Emanuella and Alexander Bigard. He was born in 1906. One brother, Sidney, is dead. Alexander Jr. still plays drums in New Orleans.

The Bigards are one of the oldest families in New Orleans, dating back to the middle 1700s. Through the lineage, there have always been musicians. Most of them played only as a hobby, however, and earned their living in fields such as cabinet-making (they were considered the most talented in the city) and cigar manufacturing. Barney's father was in the insurance business, far removed from the remote ancestor who buccaneered with Jean Lafitte.

Trumpeter Buddy Petite led the first big-time New Orleans band in which Barney played. He soon achieved mastery of the clarinet. About that time, the saxophone was becoming a favored instrument among musicians and audiences, and Barney switched to tenor. Again, he showed such promise that the word spread to Chicago and cornetist Joe (King) Oliver.

When Oliver got a contract to open at the Royal Garden in Chicago (formerly the Lincoln Gardens), he started looking for new sidemen. His original men had been snapped up by other bandleaders like Erskine Tate, Dave Peyton, and Charlie Cook, who could pay more than Joe.

Oliver, going back to the source, wrote friends in New Orleans to recommend young, talented musicians who would play for less than the Chicago fellows. Barney was high on the list of recommendations, and in the fall of 1924, he went off to Chicago to play with Oliver. He was hired as a tenor saxophonist, but when Albert Nicholas and Omer Simeon left, Oliver remembered that Barney played clarinet and bought him an instrument. From then on, Barney doubled on tenor and clarinet.

When Bigard and the other young New Orleanians arrived in Chicago from the South, considerable resentment arose among local musicians over the imported competition. This attitude may or may not have been responsible for the mysterious fire that burned the Royal Garden to the ground. In any case, the new musicians were left in a rough spot, looking for work in the strange city.

At this point Barney credits fate. Omer Simeon, then working mostly with Jelly Roll Morton, left Morton for Charlie Elgar. So Barney started playing with Jelly Roll on record dates and one-nighters, earning a living until Oliver could get started again.

When Oliver opened at the Plantation Club, Bigard was with him and, as he tells it, had his first close-up of the gangster scene. One Saturday night, the place was crowded with the usual throng —shipping clerks and their girls from the north side, pimps and race-track hustlers, fresh-faced housewives and spouses from suburban Oak Park. Then, as if by magic, the dance floor cleared, and four men slow-walked through an aisle of people. Barney says he didn't realize that the men in front were being herded out of the place at gun point—until they passed the bandstand. Then, he says, he got so frightened he grabbed his horns and ran home, where he stayed until Luis Russell, Oliver's pianist, came and got him. Later, he saw newspaper pictures of the people he had seen being ushered from the club. They were quite dead.

During those Chicago days, Barney also recalls a place called Dreamland. This was a huge ballroom that boasted three bands. The featured orchestra was that of the illustrious Doc Cook. He led an eighteen-piece group, then the largest Negro dance band in the world. There were sixteen instrumentalists held together by two drummers, one of whom was the famed Jimmy Bertrand. Cook offered Barney a job with this band, but Bigard refused, explaining that he felt more at home with Joe Oliver. There were obviously strong rapport and great mutual admiration between the two New Orleans musicians. And when Joe headed east in 1927, Barney was with him. On the way to New York City, the band, as Barney vividly remembers, became stranded in St. Louis after leaving Chicago. They were bailed out by the management of New York's Savoy Ballroom so they could open there as scheduled.

Oliver's 1927 Savoy band consisted of Red Allen, Oliver, trumpets; Jimmy Archey, trombone; Albert Nicholas, reeds; Luis Russell, piano; Pops Foster, bass; Paul Barbarin, drums; and Bigard.

After the Savoy engagement, pianist Russell took the group into the Nest Club, where Barney remained until bassist Wellman Braud induced him to join Duke Ellington in 1928. Barney did not want to leave Russell because the tips in the Nest Club were so good, but Braud painted a great musical future for the Ellington band and persuaded Barney to make the change.

When Barney became part of the Ellington organization, there were lots of excellent clarinet players around New York. Buster Bailey was with Fletcher Henderson; Prince Robinson held down both the clarinet and tenor saxophone solo posts with Elmer Snowden at the Nest Club; William Thornton Blue, with an inimitable buzz style, was featured with the Missourians (which later became Cab Calloway's orchestra); Jerry Blake was with Chick Webb; and a Cuban wizard with the improbable name of Carmelita Jejo dazzled audiences at Small's Sugar Cane Club.

At the time, Duke's band was an unknown quantity for Harlem's musicians because the crime syndicate, which operated the Cotton Club where Duke played, made no exceptions in its lily-white customer policy. A black man was forbidden to darken the Cotton Club door. Therefore, we musicians heard the Washingtonians only on records—not that we habitués of the Rhythm Club cared. As a matter of fact, Ellington at that period meant little to us, and the newspaper ads proclaiming all that "jungle jazz" show stuff irritated Harlem so much that the public and the tooters alike ignored the existence of the club—and the Duke.

This was the attitude until Duke came out with a record of his tune *Jig Walk*. It was his first recorded effort and a hit in Harlem, though lots of folks took exception to the title. They used the word jig in a fraternal sense among themselves and were offended when it was employed as a song title. But the musicians loved the record. It wasn't too much later that Barney made his first record with Ellington, which, he recalls, was *Bugle Call Rag*.

When the clarinet players found out that Bigard had come out with an unorthodox way of swinging on the instrument, they all wanted to get him in a session to see if they could cut him (or steal what they could). This was easier desired than accomplished, since, with the exception of trombonist Joe (Tricky Sam) Nanton and trumpeter Bubber Miley, the Ellingtonians were rarely caught sitting in at a jam session. Drummer Sonny Greer and his sidekick, altoist Otto (The Baron) Hardwick, were at the bars nightly, but no jamming ever interferred with their relaxation periods—that was for peasants, according to Toby Hardwick.

Finally, one night we were all standing at the bar in Big John's Saloon, where most cats congregated, when Jonesy, a Cotton Club waiter who doubled as Ellington's band valet, came in. He proclaimed that Ellington had the greatest band in the world and was the King of Harlem. All the musicians stopped talking and listened with amusement as Jonesy continued that there were no trumpet players in town to compare with Bubber Miley. Several heads nodded acknowledgement while grins grew broader.

Jonesy went down the list of fellows in Duke's band until everybody in the place became bored. We knew the capabilities of the Washingtonians. But when Barney Bigard's name was mentioned, everyone looked blank. Bigard? Nobody seemed to know him. But it happened that Happy Caldwell, the Chicago tenor saxophonist, popped in then and told us that, in his opinion, Barney played great clarinet.

William Thornton Blue spoke up, saying to Jonesy, "Well, if your man is so great, you tell him to be in the Rhythm Club with his horn, and I'll show him how to play it."

Such public challenges were rare, but sure enough, the next night the Rhythm Club was packed. Blue told Bobby Henderson, an up-and-coming piano man, to play *The World Is Waiting for the Sunrise* in a very fast tempo. Then Blue proceeded to play the devil out of the song, swinging with his familiar growl (a vibration emanating from the throat that Benny Goodman learned from Blue during Harlem jam sessions).

On this night, old Blue was blowing in extra fine form. He took over the house until. . . . It was Barney's turn. He damn near split our eardrums, opening his chorus with a wild, screaming high note, which he held all through the first chorus. Then he played the second chorus with lots of what Ellington later called "waterfalls," which I can only describe as sounding like chromatics, except that when one analyzes the passages, they prove not to be true chromatics at all.

Barney glissed, swooped, soared, making his clarinet smoke to the point that Blue packed up his horn and said, "Well, Barney, I guess Jonesy was telling the truth. I'll be in Big John's, and the drinks are on me."

Barney's Ellington days started at a time when all the guys were young and full of animal spirits, which came out not only in their music but also in the form of pranks they played on each other.

There was the time the arrangement called for Wellman Braud to make a quick switch from his string bass to tuba. At the crucial moment, Braud, unaware that Barney had filled the upright bass to the brim with water, blew a cascade of H_2O down on the sax section, with Barney catching most of the deluge.

There was the stink-bomb episode, contributed by a brother who shall remain nameless. This, according to Bigard, happened on the stage of the Pearl Theater in Philadelphia.

With rapt attention, they were accompanying a famous female singer when, as she reached her shining moment at the end of the song, a faint aroma of something quite unpleasant was detected onstage. As it grew stronger, guys started looking accusingly at each other, trying hard to preserve a dignified appearance. But the tension increased as the odor mounted, until there was no containing the mirth. Then, noticing a vacant chair, they had the answer, for the absent musician was noted for his stink-bomb jokes. Revenge was in order, so later on, the culprit's tuxedo was doused with itching powder. The combination of those oldtime klieg lights onstage and the powder soon had the guy in agony. And the air was clear from then on.

In addition to joining in the jollity, Barney also was inspired to create melodies during those Ellington days. Among the credits he claims are *Mood Indigo, Saratoga Swing, Minuet in Blue, Saturday Night Function, Stompy Jones, Clouds in My Heart, Rockin' in Rhythm*. There are many others, too, that he sold or gave away.

In 1942 he left the Ellington band to join pianist Freddy Slack. He stayed with Slack's band a year or two, then played a while with Kid Ory, and in 1946 joined Louis Armstrong, working with him off and on for some fifteen years. While with Satchmo, he toured the world and made many observations. He recalled playing theaters in the southern United States where Negroes were afraid to show appreciation until the white audiences indicated it was good. Later, he found a similar situation in Africa, where the tribal chief's approval apparently was as necessary as the white people's in the South.

Today, Bigard is semiretired because he's tired of travel. However, he always enjoys playing at sessions and college dates, if they are not too far from his home in Los Angeles. He and his wife, Dorthe are frequently visited by the children of his earlier marriage—Barney Jr., Wini, Patricia, and Marlene, plus eleven grandchildren.

Jazz of today is Barney's pet peeve. He says it does not employ melody and sacrifices rhythm just to be different. He also says he feels that if this continues, jazz will continue to die.

Barney's playing differs from any other clarinetist's in that he does not play orthodox harmonic lines. His tone ranges from a keening wail in the upper register down to a somber, rich, dark-hued tone. Bigard is an artist of tremendous facility. He is a virile, creative instrumentalist. To an acute listener, clarinet by Bigard creates a broad expanse of melodic excitement, a departure that soars fresh and warm from his soul.

Down Beat, September 8, 1966

The Frog and Me
(Ben Webster)

I RESENT THE treatment that musicians customarily are given by the press and other news media. The reporting, especially if the person is well known, is so often biased and slanted. Though sugar-coating distorts the picture and robs the subject of a semblance of reality, at the same time, gossip and inaccurate reporting can equally twist the facts. To a degree, Ben Webster has suffered this misfortune. It is my intention to examine the diverse, and sometimes contradictory, facets of Webster.

Ben Webster is not only one of the greatest exponents of the tenor saxophone but he is also a talented arranger, composer, billiard player, and photographer. Each of these things Ben does almost well enough to be considered a professional if he decided to work at any one of them. Still, throughout his career, he has followed a destiny as a communicator on his instrument. Everything else has been relegated to a hobby.

With an intriguing character that, at times, is almost Jekyll and Hyde, Ben is a strange one. This duality, of course, exists within everyone to some degree, but in his case, it is remarkable. However, I have noted these extreme shifts in more than one musician, and for some reason, they follow a pattern. I am struck by the similarities between Ben and Thelonious Monk, for example. Both, when in good spirits and in a congenial atmosphere, can break into a sort of ritual dance, consisting of a series of short glides, a shuffle, with an occasional tap thrown in. They also present a similarly morose attitude when unhappy.

The personality similarity persists even to playing the piano. This is not to imply that Ben is in a class with Monk on the instrument, since Webster does not play a really acceptable professional piano. Yet it is common knowledge that he loves to play the instrument. Ben plops himself on a piano stool every chance he gets.

According to historians, Webster started his professional career as a pianist with a man named Dutch Campbell. This may be true, but, if so, it must have been a pretty rugged outfit even for those times, since Ben's playing is confined to a honky-tonk stride style.

This was typical Kansas City barroom piano that Ben had heard from the time he was a small lad. According to most Kansas City musicians, the customary gathering place was the corner of Eighteenth and Vine. The town was wide open in those days, and there was a concentration of various restaurants, pool halls, pawnshops, and speakeasies, plus other assorted places of questionable business around this intersection. It's where the sports, pool hustlers, pimps, and musicians could be found, and there were lots of ragtime piano players around for Webster to pattern himself after.

I can sense what it must have been like, since there was the same scene in my home town, Washington, D.C., during that period of the early twenties. How intriguing that type of atmosphere was to a youngster as he lurked around the fringes of the big fellows' conversations, all eyes and ears, trying to pick up on the mysteries of life! I can remember the agony I went through trying to be a part of the gang on the corner. It took some doing. First came the fighting, which was the initiation for all youngsters.

Ben had special problems to overcome—he was the only male in a household of females, who had dressed him better and taught him to speak with more polish than the other youngsters. Children being quick to resent anyone who is different, the street corner understandably was a traumatic introduction to the other side of life for young Benjamin Francis Webster.

Born February 27, 1909, in Kansas City, Missouri, Ben was a product of the wild prohibition days. It may explain why he has tried to project the image of a tough guy until the facade became so much a part of him that few people regard him as anything other than a brusque, loud-talking fellow who loves his liquor. However, underneath this contrived image lies a warm, thoughtful, kindly person. Ben is hung up on the ambivalence of his inner self and the man he wants the world to think he is (which, I assure you, is only a cover).

For years, as far as I was concerned, the tender, warm side of Frog, as he is called by his intimates, was never apparent. I knew him only as a good drinking companion, a hell of a musician, and a swimming buddy. So when I had occasion to go to his home in Los Angeles years later, I was astounded to observe the love and affection with which he regarded his gentle little mother, a former schoolteacher, and his grandmother. The two elderly women were quiet-spoken and refined. With them, Ben was the soul of solicitude. He even combed his grandmother's hair!

Watching him with the family, it dawned on me that there was another side to this man I had prided myself on knowing so well. He also made me aware that he was my real friend, by looking after me when I arrived on the West Coast. If the going was rough for me, Ben put some money in my pocket, and he'd take me on the occasional gig that popped up. When we played golf, he always picked up the tab. These generous gestures came from his heart, not from my asking him for help.

Then, looking back, I recalled that this regard and concern were not confined to me. I remember very well how many of his other friends all over the country, particularly in New York City and Los Angeles, always received the same consideration.

One of these friends, O. D. Thompson, or Slats, as Ben always calls him, has proved an invaluable source of material in this recapitulation. They grew up together in Kansas City. Slats played in Ben's first band (later, Ben had quartets and combos from time to time), and they have been friends through the years.

Slats recalls that early band, which they called Rooster Ben and His Little Red Hens. At that time, Webster was playing that honky-tonk piano of his, after going through the motions of violin lessons and playing clarinet in the high school orchestra. These striplings started playing for youngsters' dances after school and worked their way up until they began to compete with George Lee's band and other local, established groups.

Then, all of a sudden, the town got too small for Ben, so he cut out for Albuquerque, New Mexico, with Clarence Love. He subsequently worked for Jap Allen, Gene Coy, and Dutch Campbell. Then Lester Young's father engaged him to play with the Young family band. Were it not for this, Ben might never have learned the tenor saxophone. It was Lester who introduced him to the instrument (he'd started on alto) and tutored him. The two of them would go down to the river and blow by the hour.

One day, the lessons were almost broken off for good when Lester decided to dive into the river, although he was not a good swimmer. I have never been able to find out the exact facts—whether Lester got beyond his depth, had a cramp, or what—but

Ben had to jump in and save his life. This was a feat that he was to repeat years later, rescuing someone he didn't know. These acts are unknown to most people, and Webster makes no attempt to show the better side of himself.

The person Ben was most devoted to outside of his mother and grandmother was the late Jimmy Blanton. It was Ben who first heard the young bass player and hounded Duke Ellington until he went to hear this phenomenal musician. After that, history was made. Jimmy developed the modern style of bass playing. Ben was a different man as he watched over Blanton like a mother hen. For the first time since I'd known Ben, he cut way down on his whiskey and would sit by the hour counseling young Jimmy on the facts of life. It is mere speculation—and I may be wrong —but I can't help feeling that if Blanton had followed Ben's advice, he might still be with us.

A humorous bit of the association between Blanton and Ben comes to mind. The Ellington band was up in the far northern part of the country playing a theater, and just as we finished our last show, we noticed that it had begun to snow like mad. Everybody decided to head for home immediately, instead of making one of the jam sessions that was our customary after-work amusement. I recall going to bed without stopping to eat, only to be awakened by hunger pangs a few hours later. I got up and stumbled through the blizzard to a nearby restaurant. As I drew near, I saw a strange sight. At first there appeared to be a group of primitive monsters trudging through the snow. But it was Ben carrying Blanton piggy back, with Jimmy's bass fiddle under one arm. Jimmy was doggedly hanging onto Ben's neck with one arm, while the other clutched Ben's saxophone.

I don't believe I ever have seen any two musicians closer to each other than those two. There was mutual admiration for one another as musicians and a sturdy friendship that I think permitted Jimmy to give Ben the nickname Frog. It fit well enough, what with Ben's slightly protruding eyes, to become permanent among his friends. Ben is a fairly tall, broad-shouldered man, with a definite Indian cast to his face, and a reddish-brown coloring. In recent years, his hair has begun to recede, and his huge chest has gracefully slid below his waist.

The first time I saw Ben was when I was with Horace Henderson's Collegians of Wilberforce University. We had returned to school after being on tour during summer vacation, and lack of sleep and irregular meals had exhausted us bandsmen. So instead of joining the other upperclassmen in the hazing and usual initiation festivities, we all went to bed right after supper. Later, we were rudely awakened by a sound that seemed to be a cross between the mating call of a bull moose and the frightened honking of a southbound goose that has lost its bearings. Everybody jumped up and ran to the window. Looking out, we saw a big gang of fellow students surrounding a fellow sitting on a tree stump, blowing either an alto or soprano saxophone. The next morning when we asked about the commotion, we found out that freshman Ben Webster from Kansas City had avoided being paddled by blowing the sax.

No doubt we would have gotten to know Webster better, but soon after that meeting, the Collegians decided to leave school permanently. The next time our paths crossed was years later.

When Ben arrived in New York City, all the tenor playing cats around town were talking about his big sound. I remember there was quite a bit of plotting and planning by the musicians as they tried to inveigle Webster into a cutting session. Ben had no eyes for that kind of action. He'd be in and out of the Rhythm Club or other spots where Chu Berry, Elmer Williams, Happy Caldwell, Big Nick Nicholas, and the other tenors hung out. They'd be jamming, but Ben would just sip and listen.

I well remember hearing of an incident that took place just about that time. I heard it from one of Ben's boon companions, a fellow whom I knew only as Slim. He told me that early one morning, while they were getting the air in Slim's car, on Harlem River Drive, a young woman jumped into the river. Ben yelled to Slim to stop the car, and as soon as he did, Ben dived in, clothes and all, and saved her. Ben is modest; he even denies remembering this incident.

Later in our friendship, I discovered that Ben was equally skilled with a pool cue. One night in the Rhythm Club, I heard him challenge one of the gambling fraternity who frequented the place. All the musicians knew that this fellow (who shall remain nameless) was a pool hustler, so we tried to dissuade Ben from betting money against him. But once Ben has made up his mind there's no stopping him.

The game was on—"fifty no count," meaning that the winning player had to run fifty balls (that's three racks plus five balls). They tossed a coin and the pool hustler lost. He had to break the balls, which he did very professionally, making the two end balls touch a cushion and then return to the stack, leaving Ben's cue ball in Siberia against the far cushion.

We all expected Ben to retaliate by playing safe, which would have been the smart thing to do, with ten bucks at stake. But not Kansas City Ben—he'd hung around with Odelle and Piney Brown on Eighteenth and Vine too long to let a little thing like Siberia faze him. He said something like: "Gee whiz, you sure are hard on a man, leaving him safe like this on the very first shot. My, my. What am I supposed to do from here? Tell you what— I'll give you two dollars, and let's start all over. Okay?" As he made these and other choice remarks, much too salty to repeat, he circled the table looking for a possible combination.

Ben squatted for a few seconds, got up, and yelled, "Rackman, don't go away! There's going to be some balls to be racked in a minute." Then he called a ball in the stack in the left corner pocket. (This shot, we thought, was impossible because it was a two-cushion combination bank shot.) Ben made it. Then he proceeded to run the table, three racks, plus five balls and out.

According to Odelle and Montell Stewart, who grew up with him in Kansas City, Ben came by his skill on the green naturally, because as a yearling he was happiest when he hung out with them as they loafed around the pool hall at Twelfth and Paseo —until they all discovered that girls were more fun.

Ben was quite a daredevil in his younger days. As a joke, he once thumped Joe Louis on the button while riding an elevator in the old Brill Building. Few people would have had the temerity to trifle with the champ, but Ben figured he knew him well enough to kid around—Louis was an Ellington fan. However, the Brown Bomber was not amused and returned a tiny jab to Ben's ribs, doubling him up.

I was not present, but I've heard another story from several fellows who were there. Ben once challenged Keg O'Nails, a gent who had a terrible temper, wore two guns, and enjoyed whipping a joker's head, which he did with impunity since he was a policeman. Inviting Keg to step outside, Ben spiced his threats with impolite name-calling. However, a good fairy must have been watching over him because the policeman refused to take offense, and, laughing, bought Frog a drink. They became fast friends and soon were patrolling Keg's beat together.

One year, when the Ellingtonians were in Denver, Barney Bigard, Ben, and I each had rings custom-made by a goldsmith. Barney and I still have ours, but Ben's underwent constant changes of ownership because of his attraction to "the church."

Some of Ben's Chicago cronies introduced him to "the church." Although these "churchgoers" often knelt to pray, it was over dice—this former house of worship had become the scene of one of the biggest crap games in Chicago. We fellows in the band could always tell when Ben had been to "church" and also if it had been a good or bad session. The clue was Ben's pinky finger. If his snake ring adorned his hand, he had won and was in good financial shape. But if he was not wearing it, disaster had set in during the game and the snake was in pawn again. Eventually, it disappeared forever.

Nobody seeing Ben hanging out on the corner of Forty-seventh and South Park, or Eighteenth and Vine, or at the Braddock Bar in Harlem would ever suspect that he was anything other than a corner roustabout. His yelling and laughing fit right into the picture, as did his attire. His high-priced shoes were just like those affected by gamblers, hustlers, and pimps, while his expensive hats were worn cocked in such a manner that they were a blatant gesture of defiance to the conventional world. Somehow

his headgear always seemed to antagonize lawmen, who'd spot
Ben and invariably stop him and request identification.

Is Ben Webster saint or sinner? Sometimes his behavior borders
on the eccentric, and, as we all know, musicians are placed in an
atmosphere where the sauce flows. For Webster, in an attempt to
be sociable, this represents a continuing battle with the bottle
(which he has been known to lose). On the other side of the
coin, Ben has been kind and generous in situations where most
fellows would just refuse to get involved.

I recall one incident as an example. It was around 7:00 a.m.
in a theatrical rooming house, and it was snowing outside. Inside,
there were vague rumblings heard, like someone moving furni-
ture. The noise woke everybody up, but it soon grew quiet again.
Later, it was discovered that there had indeed been some furni-
ture moving as a certain band brother had shoved the bed, the
dresser, and several tables between himself and his irate spouse.

The summary of this touching domestic scene came to light
when this brother caught up with the band again in Chicago, two
days later. He was wearing Ben's clothing, including shoes and
hat. Good Samaritan Webster had helped the brother out with
both clothing and money.

There are some parallels between Ben's playing and his personal life. Over the years, his style has undergone a complete
turnabout, which is obvious to a discerning listener. During his
early period, he blew with unrestrained savagery, buzzing and
growling through chord changes like a prehistoric monster chal-
lenging a foe. With the passage of time, this fire has given way to
tender, introspective declamations of such maturity and reflective
beauty that he has acquired a large number of new fans all over
the world.

Among those of us who knew him, there was considerable baf-
flement when his style changed, but the question was answered
to my satisfaction as I started this article and the facts began to
assemble themselves. Ben has returned to his cultural roots, by
chance or design. In either case, these latest musical extensions
are not in keeping with the mores of his former hoodlum companions.

Red Norvo, far right, *and his band on 52nd Street*

Coleman Hawkins in the early sixties

Ben Webster

The John Kirby band at a recording session, left to right, *Billy Kyle, Buster Bailey, Russ Procope, Charlie Shavers, O'Neil Spencer, John Kirby*

Harry Carney and Billy Strayhorn

The Ellington Trombones, left to right, *Joe (Tricky Sam) Nanton, Juan Tiz*
Lawrence Brown

Art Tatum on piano

Louis Armstrong in the early thirties

Benny Carter makes a point

Fletcher Henderson, seated, and Rex Stewart, 1932

Duke Ellington conducts bodily and musically from the piano

Jo Jones, Count Basie, Walter Paige, Buck Clayton

Rex Stewart in the forties

Fortunately, Ben has recorded extensively, so that gamut, from rough to mellow, is available to the jazz buff. He played with many bands, recording with most of them. He was with Bennie Moten, Blanche Calloway, Fletcher Henderson, Benny Carter, Cab Calloway, Raymond Scott, Teddy Wilson, and Duke Ellington. He also recorded with Art Tatum, Billie Holiday, and other pickup groups.

As a composer and arranger, Ben's most significant contribution was *Cotton Tail*, for which he also wrote the now-famous saxophone-section chorus.

Ben is a nonconformist. He has developed a personality facade that is the antithesis of what he is, for Ben is also warm and generous, a true friend, a great musician, and—taking into account the total picture—a tremendous human being. I fail to understand why a distinction should be made between his behavior in a public bar and that of a celebrated Welsh poet who was such a cutup a few years ago. The latter's antics did not tarnish his image as an artistic force. The fact that a fellow earns a living as a musician should not condemn him.

It is my hope that in Europe, where he has lived and worked for the last few years, he will find the inner peace that his restless soul seeks. Viva Ben Webster, our Frog.

Down Beat, June 1, 1967

Harry Carney: Boss Baritone

HARRY HOWELL CARNEY is the name, and for more than forty years his contributions to the world of jazz have earned him great fame and have made his name synonymous with the baritone saxophone. As a general rule, when an instrumentalist really makes it big, everybody tries to imitate him. However, Carney's conception is unique, so personalized that no one has been able successfully to copy his style or his famous sonority on the baritone saxophone. Therefore, Harry remains ensconced in the upper echelons and stands like a mountain in his field.

His saga begins in Boston, where he was a member of the Knights of Pythias boys band, playing clarinet. He proved so adept on this instrument that he acquired an alto saxophone as well and soon was proficient enough on both horns to attract the attention of Henry Sapro, a friend of the family. Sapro played banjo, and upon obtaining an engagement in New York, asked the Carney family if he could take young Harry along.

As a yearling, Harry was the personification of shyness and was most unworldly. Nevertheless, when the engagement ended, he elected to stay in New York. Thanks to the many proper Bostonians who had preceded him on the Harlem musical scene, Carney was well bodyguarded by such older fellows as Willie Lynch and Bobby Sawyer until he'd learned the ropes in the Apple.

During those times, good alto saxophones were in plentiful supply around the Rhythm Club, and strangely enough, quite a few of them were from Beantown and boyhood chums of Harry's. For example, there was Johnny (Little Caesar) Hodges and the gifted Charlie Holmes. Both of these chaps grew up in the same neighborhood as Harry. Then, there was Hilton Jefferson, another talented New Englander, who had come from Providence, Rhode Island, with the Julian Arthur burlesque band and stayed on to compete in New York alongside a flock of other up-and-coming tooters who were setting the pace in Harlem—Benny Carter, Eugene Fields, and Russell Procope.

Our friendship began so long ago that neither Harry nor I is able to recall the exact date when we first met. However, we do both agree as to the circumstances, which occurred when we were both kids.

Somewhere between late 1923 and early 1924, I was a member of Leon Abbey's Savoy Bearcats, the house orchestra at the famous New York ballroom. As I recall, we were booked into a ballroom in Boston for a weekend. (This engagement sticks in my mind because it was the first time that I had ever been in that city, and I was curious about the good people of Beantown.) Our drummer, Willie Lynch, was a Bostonian and had what seemed to us fellows an affected way of speech, with broad a's and other Britishisms. We all wondered if other Bostonians spoke this way too.

At the ballroom, we were a great success, and many of the local musicians were in attendance. Standing right in front of the bandstand was a tall, brown-skinned beanpole of a kid, who watched our clarinet star, Carmelito Jejo, with tremendous concentration. No one in the band paid any particular attention to the fellows around the bandstand, except to be amused at Jejo's admirer. We were all too busy winking and blinking at the pretty little girls while wondering about the blue laws of Boston.

The lawmen, according to rumor, were quite dedicated to preserving the public morals and worked vigorously to make certain that no hanky-panky or smooching took place. The way we heard it, if a fellow was caught in any compromising scene, there were only two alternatives—marry the girl or go to jail. This may or may not have been the law. I wouldn't know, being too much of a coward to have tested it.

In any case, after the dance, we were all introduced to Harry by George Tynes, whom we had known in New York. We headed for Shag Taylor's drugstore, that being the out-of-town musicians hangout (this being prohibition days), and Shag, if he was in a good mood, would pass out some fine soothing syrup.

The next time I saw Carney, he was in New York with Sapro for the engagement at the ill-fated Bamboo Inn, located on Seventh Avenue in Harlem. Sapro's group was ousted by a fire that closed the joint—on opening night, as I recall. Meanwhile, Harry had taken to hanging out at the Rhythm Club, as did everybody else and his brother, to fraternize and hope for a gig at the same time. Carney and I played a lot of pool together in those days.

When Cecil Benjamin, our clarinetist with the Johnny Montague Band (of which I was then a member), took off without any warning, I called Harry for the gig, which was in a dancing school downtown on Twenty-third Street. This job didn't last too long for either one of us, and neither Harry nor I recall whether we quit or were fired.

Harry is a bit hazy as to his exact activities following the Montague engagement, but I have the feeling it wasn't too much later that he joined Duke, for what has probably become the longest engagement any musician ever had with any bandleader.

Ellington's saxophone section at that time was composed of Otto Hardwick, first alto, and Rudy Jackson, tenor, and Harry joined to play third alto and clarinet. I vaguely remember Bob Robinson taking the tenor saxophone spot for a while, but that can't have lasted very long. Band personnels were not very stable in those days, and fellows were constantly jumping from band to band. This was partly caused by the economics of the business —but most bandleaders were also constantly on the lookout to find better sidemen to strengthen their groups. Also, sometimes there was a personal reason for one bandleader's attempt to raid the band of another leader.

Most people have long ago forgotten the feud that used to exist between Elmer Snowden and Duke Ellington. The schism began after Snowden had brought Ellington to New York as his sideman and the young Duke subsequently wound up as leader of the same group. Thereafter, the rift grew wider every time they exchanged places on the Kentucky Club bandstand. Wherever Snowden played (during the years that I was with him), Duke would always turn up, and sometime during the evening (out of Elmer's hearing, of course), Ellington would go into his half-kidding, half-serious act. Duke would call aside one of the musicians (Jimmy Harrison for example) and the conversation was always the same—I can still quote it verbatim: "So-and-so, when are you going to stop fooling around and join a *real* band?"

This was the spiel that Ellington laid on the three guys that he tried to win away—trombonist Harrison, tenor saxophonist Prince

Robinson (also clarinet), and especially Joe Garland, whom Duke courted assiduously for his baritone stompability. Harry's role in this drama becomes apparent when it is known that both Harrison and Robinson did play with Duke for a short time, while Garland never succumbed.

Ellington always wanted that depth of the baritone sound, so when he enlarged his group for the Cotton Club engagement, he immediately switched Carney to baritone. Neither Harry nor Duke could have guessed that this casual arrangement would turn out to be a lifetime career, or that Harry's work on the baritone would become an international influence. Perhaps because of the structure of the instrument, with its not inconsiderable bulk and weight, there always has been a scarcity of really proficient performers. "The beast," as Johnny Barnes, the English baritone star, affectionately labels his instrument, does not have the general appeal to a budding musician that a smaller instrument like the alto or tenor has. One can just about count on two hands the outstanding individuals, stylewise, on the baritone—and have a few fingers left over.

Among those whom I feel worthy of mention was, of course, the exciting booting baritone man with Pops Snowden—Joe Garland, who well may have been the start of it all.* It was his sound that caused Duke to incorporate that sound, with Harry, in his band.

Then there was a very original fellow who played in pianist Willie Gant's band at the then new Small's Paradise, whom I only remember as Horsecollar. This lad attacked his old Conn like he was a ferocious lion mangling his prey. Horsecollar was a strong, shouting player, but he lacked finesse. I can't ignore the artistry of Ernie Caceres, the Mexican-American virtuoso, on the instrument. Also worthy of mention is Pepper Adams and the previously mentioned Johnny Barnes, who sparked the Alex Welsh band with whom I toured England last summer. Another of the fellows who moves me is Bill Hood, who makes Los Angeles his home

---

* Garland later became well known as an arranger, and as the composer of *In the Mood*.

and can be heard in the section of many a television or motion picture group.

I've purposely saved mention of Gerry Mulligan for last because, as I see it, this ebullient elf of the instrument bridges the gap between yesterday and today. Mulligan, with his imagination, skill, and verve, has outpaced the majority of his fellows in many respects and is indeed a consummate artist. Nevertheless, standing like Horatio at the bridge, there's the figure of Harry Carney, who, to me, represents the ultimate on this horn.

Measured by any scale of appraisal, Carney is quite a fellow, and in so many ways over and above his well-known musical capabilities. He is cultured, knowledgeable, and also blessed with such an abundance of good nature that he enriches most scenes by his presence, a factor that has benefited the profession, Ellington, and himself. This attribute has been confirmed and proved by the vast multitude of friends and fans all over the world who regard Carney highly.

Under most circumstances, such a sweeping statement could be regarded with a jaundiced eye—or as a press agent's ploy for publicity. But in the case of Harry Carney, the truth is the light, and this chap emerges as a paragon of virtues. As a matter of fact, this profile posed problems, because Harry is an individual who lacks the human frailties that make up the color and personality of most musicians. What can one say about a man who always does his job in a most professional manner? Harry is the one who is first on the bandstand, tuning up his horn, and the last fellow to leave after the set (or the evening) is over, having carefully packed up his instruments. Also, when Ellington's orchestra takes a break, it is Carney who smilingly chitchats with people from the audience, signs autographs, and briefs the fans as to where the band is headed or has arrived from.

As a reaffirmation of his regard for people, when the mood strikes him, he will get on the phone and spend hours calling all over the country to his friends. He carries several little address books with him, and his friends can expect to hear from Harry some time during the year, but certainly at Christmastime. It is rumored that Harry's Christmas card list numbers in the thousands.

Another of his pleasures (at least when I was also with Duke) was photography. Harry and Otto Hardwick, the impeccable former first saxophone player of the Ellington organization, had a mythical photographic firm with trunks of equipment—at least several thousands of dollars worth of enlargers, cameras, gadgets, and film—and were constantly involved in photography. Only the firm, for which cards were printed reading "Hardwick and Carney—We Aim to Tease" or "Pick a Flock of Pickled Pictures. P.S. Bring Your Own Pickles, We're Pickled Enough Already," was nonexistent. They didn't make much money, but they had a lot of fun.

Developed in later years was another of Harry's hobbies, driving a big Imperial all over the country, usually accompanied by Duke. This, of course, was prior to the Ellingtonians' really far-flung traveling schedule, which forced the organization to fly to most engagements, but when there's driving to be done today, Carney and Duke still team up.

If it is true that early environment shapes the individual, as I happen to believe, then it becomes clear why Carney developed into such a likable human being, since he is the product of a most harmonious household. I well remember how his parents always extended themselves in making Harry's band-buddies welcome every time we played Boston.

Harry's mother, a beautiful cook, would graciously put on a feast that even now makes my mouth water, especially those codfish balls, hot rolls, and baked beans, all of which she prepared so deliciously. And those would only be part of the feast. Usually, there would be homemade strawberry shortcake in summer, or chocolate layer cake in winter. In short, any member of the group who was ever exposed to the Carney hospitality has never forgotten it.

Every now and then, happenings serve as indications of a person's character, and one unforgettable incident occurred many years ago from which Harry, in my opinion, emerged a hero.

This took place during the period when Duke's band was a red-hot attraction in Canada, and we played in that country quite frequently. One time, we began with a two-week engagement at the famous Canadian exposition, went into Buffalo, and then immediately doubled back to Toronto. However, our re-entry bore no resemblance to our departure, which had been accompanied by worshipful fans and great good will.

This time, as we pulled into the station, there were no crowds lined up to greet us. Instead, there was a line of grim-faced Mounties, who were too involved in going through our special car with a fine-toothed comb to be their usual polite selves.

To this day, I don't know what they were seeking, really, but I do seem to have heard stories to the effect that there was a tip-off concerning marijuana. Harry, to my knowledge, had never trod that primrose path, but nevertheless they singled him out for a thorough interrogation. It took a hero to endure this unpleasantness and never point a finger at the brother who, by process of elimination, could well have been the culprit—if there really had been a guilty one.

Carney, in his yearling days, was quite a trencherman, no doubt the result of the aforementioned skill of his mother in the cuisine department. Consequently, wherever the band happened to be playing—whether in Kansas City or Kokomo, Louisville or St. Louis—it was Harry who knew where to find the best food. And, even more important, what time the victuals were served.

I recall an incident that illustrates two things: how much fans think of Carney and how ingenious an empty stomach can make a fellow.

On one of the Ellingtonians' initial tours into the deep South, a snafu developed over the eating arrangements. We were traveling in style, with two Pullmans plus our own baggage car. According to the railroad setup, various dining cars were assigned to meet us at junctions, feed us, and return to the main line.

One night, we finished the job, entrained, and awakened the next morning eagerly awaiting breakfast. The train sped on—no stop, no diner—causing everybody to start beefing. Under the mounting tension, Ellington got himself up and spoke with the conductor, who halted the train at the next fair-sized town. Here, there was no restaurant in the station, and across the street the proprietor of the coffee shop refused to serve us.

Harry resourcefully consulted one of his little address books, telephoned ahead some 100 miles to a wealthy friend, explained the situation, and when we arrived at that town a tremendous meal was awaiting us.

In his younger days, Carney was in many ways just like his compatriots of those times—full of fun, vim, and vigor, especially in the sauce department. So it figures that he paid his dues, what with the hangups of being exposed to that old debbil road, accompanied by segregated accommodations, long-extended travel, bad food, and all the rest of it.

Yet, today he has the appearance of a man who has lived in nothing but comfort. It's a toss-up as to whether he's found that legendary fountain of youth or has formulated a philosophy that gives him that inner strength and serenity reflected in his youthful appearance. It is amazing that a man who has been playing uninterruptedly with Ellington since 1926 (and professionally at least three years before that) is so unmarked by time.

Harry is a rarity in so many ways. His career with Duke must set a record of some sort in the business for longevity. I personally don't know of any other individual who has remained in the same organization for such a span, always contributing, always the sturdy foundation on which the group depends.

It is also unusual to work with a fellow musician who possesses such a well-balanced outlook on life. In all the years that I have known Harry, I've never seen him lose his temper, although sometimes he has come close to doing so under extreme provocation. Somehow, he has always managed to retain control of himself.

Carney, a well-built fellow who stands about five feet eleven inches, possesses almost unbelievable stamina. I don't recall his ever being ill, and his mahogany-hued visage smiles at the world much more often than it frowns. Many of the present-day tooters could take lessons from Mr. Baritone in public relations, for Carney is a past grand master at the art. This becomes apparent once one has seen that broad smile and felt the warm graciousness that emanates from Harry as he considerately answers the interminable questions of the fans. I have often watched him snatch his horn from his mouth when he had a two-bar rest to inform someone of the title of the tune that the band was playing at the moment, while the other musicians on the front line impassively ignored the questions.

So much for his personality. Now for a commentary on the artistry of this most unusual individual. Harry, with his complete control of the baritone saxophone, has a range on the instrument that surpasses credibility. He plays the higher octaves not only in tune but with a tenderness that is sometimes mindful of a cello's sound. Then, when called for, he's able to attack the sonorous bottom of the horn with such vigor and vitality that it is small wonder he has been the anchor man in Ellington's orchestra for these many years. As any good arranger can affirm, the most important tone in a chord cluster is the bottom note. This has been Harry's key function in Ellington's scores.

In addition to being an accomplished flutist, clarinetist, bass clarinetist, and alto saxophonist, too, Harry also has contributed many original compositions to the orchestra's library. In his lighter moments, Carney loves to sing, mostly confined to warbling in the shower. However, on at least two occasions Carney has been a part of the rare Ellington group vocals. Once a trio of would-be singers—Hayes Alvis, then our bassist, Harry, and myself—did a fairly creditable job of singing a Duke opus entitled *I've Got to Be a Rug Cutter.* Then, this trio accompanied the late Ivie Anderson, providing background choral effects to an Ellington recording of *A Day at the Races* (which the band had previously played in the movie). Vintage vocalists, to be sure, but for those times, almost professional.

In examining our subject, it becomes difficult for me to differentiate between the man and his communication with the world and the musician who equally communicates. Harry Car-

ney and the baritone saxophone have become so completely identified with one another that if someone speaks his name, it immediately evokes the response "baritone saxophone." In a profession
that is overloaded with good, better, and best players, Harry Carney has been sticking out like a sore thumb, because for many
years Carney was not merely the best baritone saxophone player
in these or other parts, but as far as the world of jazz was concerned, Carney was Mr. Baritone himself. There may be a poll
that he hasn't won, but I don't know which it could be. He has
trophies, plaques, citations, and what-have-you from *Esquire,*
Melody Maker, Down Beat, Jazz Journal, and you name it.

It is to be hoped that Carney's youthful appearance and good
health are indicators that Harry will be with us for many years to
come, continuing to enrich the literature of music and displaying true humanity to the people who make the business possible
—the jazz fans.

Down Beat, November 2, 1967

Getting to Europe—and
Getting Out

BACK IN 1939, the Ellingtonians' tour of the Continent was abruptly
cut short by the ominous war clouds which were gathering and
growing more imminent daily.

Irving Mills, Ellington's manager, cancelled the rest of the tour,
and before you could say "up jumped the rabbit"—we were

headed for home via the North Sea, en route for Southampton, where we'd be able to get a fast ocean liner to New York.

The carrier was quite a reputable ship, the Ile de France, but due to some type of emergency no doubt caused by the forthcoming conflict, we were told while on board a much smaller vessel that there'd be a two-day layover in London, which cheered everybody up no end and intrigued me personally since I had never before set foot on British soil, with the exception of Canada.

Arriving at some port I can no longer recall, we whisked through customs, boarded a train for London as Tricky Sam Nanton (the king of the growl trombone) kept all the band's newer fellows in stitches, laughing at his approximation of cockney rhyming slang, which he assured us was the real McCoy, direct from Bow Bells.

We had a most enjoyable holiday and took leave of the city with deep regret, since everyone we met was so warm and friendly, so kind and knowledgeable about the Duke, his men, and his music.

The comedy relief for the hour of parting was provided by the great, grand Sonny Greer and his sidekick "Baron" Toby Hardwick, who, when he was not wearing his famed monocle answered to just plain everyday Toby, erstwhile lead saxophone in the organization.

Everybody boarded the boat train, hung over from various bon voyage parties or whatever, and I remember being shaken awake by Jonesy, our invaluable man of all things. And as Jonesy asked where I had seen Greer last, I couldn't recall; nor did I remember sighting the Baron, which was understandable, since I also was rather bust myself.

We disembarked from the train, boarded the Ile de France, were assigned our cabins, and still no word of the missing pair.

As departure time drew near, tension mounted as the fellows began to worry out loud, speculating, conjecturing and wondering what had happened to Toby and Greer.

Edward Kennedy Ellington was perhaps the most relaxed person in his entourage. As he said: "There's no problem; they'll make it somehow, even if they have to con some German submarine into letting them off in New York harbor."

Duke knew his hometown buddies all right, though at the time I didn't believe him. However, just as the hoarse voice of the liner was proclaiming "I'm on my way!" there came a shrill insistent tooting from out in the fog.

After a few seconds of this Alphonse-Gaston dialogue, which was evidently some sort of ship-talk code, the fog lifted a bit, and we saw a tiny pilot boat sidle up to the monster Ile de France.

We watched with considerable awe the sight of the Baron, all decked out in top hat, monocle, and with an Inverness cape covering his evening attire. He looked like a twentieth-century Napoleon as he supported Sonny Greer.

Toby, as he tottered up the improvised gangplank, called out over his shoulder, "Easy with that case of champagne, my man."

Sonny, still wearing his grin, laboriously made his way, and when he finally got aboard he gave Duke a real military salute and said: "Well now, Governor, that was nice timing." Then he fell flat on his face.

This episode is just one among many I shall always retain as a segment, a portion of the montage of mirth, melody and magic of those Ellington days.

Another phase of my life began when World War II finally drew to a weary conclusion, and I started mulling over the possibilities of doing better for myself and family (having managed to produce three offspring in between my touring with Ellington— Helena, Regina, and Rex III).

So after much thought and prodding from my imagination, I built up enough courage to take the giant step, and as I look back upon those days I can see now what a terrible traumatic scene I was exposing myself to. But it was what I had to do at the time.

I organized an eight-man group, figuring to emulate in style what I had previously done with Duke, and much to my surprise it came off rather well, considering I didn't have my former Ellington sidekicks to boot me along with their wonderful skill and momentum.

For a while we had a swinging affair going, playing such places as the Apollo Theater in Harlem, the Three Deuces on Fifty-second Street, the Aquarium on Broadway, etc., until the flesh peddlers moved into the small group scene and the squeeze began.

At first I tried to join them—the agents—by pointing out the situation in Europe, where I felt the people would be most receptive to jazz. They had already proved this, plus the fact that after the damnable horror of war the climate for enjoyment was uppermost in most people's minds, running a close second to the necessities of life.

In any case, the bookers, to a man, laughed at my idea, telling me that the obstacles were insurmountable. Contracts could not be enforced, travel was uncertain, and, worst of all, there were no facilities for getting the money out of the various countries.

This attitude, coming from agents and bookers, got my dander up, so I started writing letters to people like Panassié in France, Tage Ammendrup in Iceland, Nils Hellstrom in Sweden, and shortly thereafter I went into rehearsal for my first European tour, feeling pretty cocky for having proven that I was right.

But perhaps I wouldn't have felt so smug if I had realized that the word would quickly spread around among the booking fraternity that Stewart had had the disgusting nerve to book himself into Europe.

This sort of thing could not be forgiven, I was told by a friendly impresario, years later, when he was in his cups. Which is not to imply that I had delusions of grandeur, but when I did return to the States after five years in Europe and Australia, the next gig that I found for myself was in Mexico City.

My second visit was in 1948, and the third visit has started off very beautifully, and I'd like to write my impressions. I'm unable to do so at this time because of space limitations. But I will in the very near future, and in the meantime, keep swinging.

Melody Maker, June 4, 1966

The Cutting Sessions

ODAY, FAME CAN COME swiftly on the heels of a Top Twenty record, but there was a time when a musician had to prove himself to other musicians in a cutting session. Whether a fellow hailed from New Orleans, San Francisco, Chicago, or wherever, he had to come to the center—New York—before he could get on the road to (relatively speaking) fame and fortune.

There, in the Apple, his skill was tested in competition with the established ones. If he couldn't cut the mustard, he became part of the anonymous mob; capable, perhaps, but not of star quality. However, if the critical, hardblowing jazzmen conceded him recognition, that acclaim would carry him on to bigger and better jobs.

This musical action on the New York battlefield was the cutting session, and the expression was an appropriate one. When a musician picked up his instrument, his intention was to outperform the other man. No quarter was given or expected, and the wound to a musician's ego and reputation could be as deep as a cut.

To a degree, all musicians, white or black, underwent the same test of strength. After arriving in the big town, a player first got squared away with a room. The next thing he'd do would be to ask where the musicians hung out. Downtown and in the evenings, this was usually a bar, say Charlie's Tavern. By day, it was much easier—most of the fellows could be found congregated

on the street around the offices of the musicians union, Local
802. But uptown, night or day, Bert Hall's Rhythm Club at 132nd
Street, just off Seventh Avenue in Harlem was the main testing
ground, and there most of the jamming originated.

As I recall, the process of elimination usually went this way.
Whenever a stranger popped into the Rhythm Club, somebody
would greet him with a hearty "Hi there, where are you from?"
followed by "What do you blow?" If the newcomer was carrying
his saxophone, trombone, or trumpet case, he would be invited to
blow some, or, as they said in the argot of the time, "to show out."

Some piano man—and there were always a few of them in the
place—would amble over to the keyboard and start comping a
tune like *Sweet Georgia Brown* or *Dinah*. This was the cue for the
stranger to pull out his instrument and show what he could do.
Meanwhile, the word had gone out all over the neighborhood—
"stand by!"—because if this cat was really good, it was the duty of
every tub to drop whatever he was doing and rush to the club.
And nobody ever did fall into New York City and cut the entire
field—some brother always came to the rescue of New York's
prestige.

These sessions, as every other aspect of life, had a pecking
order. The giants seldom deigned to compete with the peasantry.
Instead, they sat around getting their kicks, listening with amusement as the neophyte struggled to justify his claim to entry into
the charmed circle of the (for want of a better word) establish-
ment.

The blowing would start, and the pilgrim's status was soon
established—he was either in or out. If he was in, he would be
toasted at Big John's bar, and friendships were formed that assured his being invited to sit in a session with the big shots, who
did their serious blowing at the Hoofer's Club, downstairs in the
basement of the same building.

There, in the Hoofer's Club, the cream of the crop in New York
could be found—Jimmy and Tommy Dorsey, Benny Carter,
Frankie Trumbauer, Buster Bailey, Sidney De Paris, Fats Waller,
and just about every other great name in jazz. Almost every night,

rain, snow, or what have you, there was a session—nothing prevented the cats from getting together.

I said that no individual ever came to town and carved everybody, but there was one exception—Louis Armstrong. He was so tough on his trumpet that nobody dared challenge him. Come to think of it, I don't remember ever seeing him at a session. He didn't come to us—we had to go to him. I shall never forget the scrambling to get to one tiny window backstage at Roseland Ballroom, just to catch Satchmo putting the "heat to the beat" with Fletcher Henderson.

Nor can I forget the memorable occasion when Jelly Roll Morton swaggered up to the piano in the Rhythm Club announcing that he, the king of the ivory ticklers, was ready for all turkeys (a not-so-flattering way of referring to any possible competition). Making such a proclamation was like waving a red flag in front of a bull.

Jelly's monologue was fascinating as he comped and talked about how great he was, but after a few minutes of this performance, the first of the local piano giants, Willie (The Tiger) Gant walked in. He immediately sensed that Morton outclassed him, and after listening a while to Jelly's Kansas City rolling bass, he phoned Willie (The Lion) Smith to come right down. I don't think Jelly Roll and Willie had ever met, but the air became charged with professional animosity when The Lion hit the scene and snarled, "Either play something or get up, you heathen. The Lion is in port, and it's my mood to roar!" Such an unfriendly put-down caused Jelly to tear into a fast rag, which brought the house down. Morton, hearing the applause, looked up from the piano, sweating and beaming. Evidently he felt that there would be no contest.

The Lion, unimpressed, just pushed Jelly off the piano stool and, without breaking the rhythm of Jelly's tour de force, played one of his own rags with equal skill and just as great an impact on the audience.

The duel had taken on the aspect of a stand-off, so the call went out for Fats Waller, but Fats was nowhere to be found. Just then, the all-time boss of the Harlem stride piano players, James P. Johnson, arrived, having been advised of what was going on via the grapevine.

James P., who sometimes stuttered, said, "Jelly, come on, l-l-let's go down to the Hoofers. They have a b-b-better piano there, and I'll en-entertain you."

Jelly agreed, and everybody followed. As I recall, there were about sixty or seventy cats in the "second line" on that occasion. History was made as James P. wiped up the floor with Jelly Roll. Never before or since have I heard such piano playing!

At that time, New York was session-happy. Everybody blew at everybody. Guys were so eager not to miss an opportunity to sit in that many of them had two horns—one kept on the job and the other stashed away at the Rhythm Club or a nearby bar. Some sessions might be held in almost any corner bar, but they weren't the important ones.

One character, Jazz Curry, a bassist, was a familiar sight on Seventh Avenue, trudging up and down the street carrying both his brass and string basses, looking for another bass man to challenge. Bass contests were rare in the Rhythm Club or anywhere else.

A history-making session was the one between Thornton Blue, the Saint Louis clarinetist then with Cab Calloway, and Buster Bailey. That evening, a gang of clarinet players started noodling. I remember Blue, Russell Procope, Carmelito Jejo, Jimmy Dorsey, Benny Goodman, and many others being present (this was in the very early thirties before Benny had his band). After trying out various tunes, they agreed to play *Liza*. One by one, everybody dropped out until only Bailey and Blue remained. Blue was swinging like mad, but Buster took the honors as he increased the tempo, chorus by chorus, until you could hardly pat your foot. In those days, the late Buster Bailey could cut every living tub on the clarinet.

This was a beautiful period for the music and the players. There was little jealousy and no semblance of Jim Crow or Crow Jim in the sessions. Musicians were like fraternity brothers, despite their being aware of the distinction that was strongly maintained by white agents, bookers, and the public. The jazz-men were bound together by their love for the music—and what the rest of the world thought about fraternizing did not matter.

Among my memories, I treasure the historic confrontation that took place between the trombone giants, Jack Teagarden and Jimmy Harrison. They first met in 1927 at Roseland Ballroom in New York. That meeting remains etched firmly in my mind, since, on that night, the band was initiated into the sacred rites of what was then known as Texas Muggles. Now it is called by many other names—tea, Mary-Jane, or just plain marijuana. (I only mention this to pinpoint the occasion.) When Mr. Texas met Mr. New York, a mutual admiration society was formed at once. Jack thought that Jimmy was just about the greatest 'bone that had ever come down the pike, and Jimmy felt the same way about Jack, putting him above Miff Mole, who also was a tremen-dous trombone on that scene. I might also mention that Teagar-den was one of the few musicians, except for a few greats like Fats Waller, who ever was permitted to sit in with the Fletcher Henderson Band.

Soon Jimmy and Jack started hanging out uptown, which caused quite a few uplifted eyebrows among those Harlemites who resented Teagarden's Texas brogue and appearance. But Jimmy would declare that Jack was more Indian than Caucasian, which made everything all right, so the two buddies began to be seen quite a bit, especially in the King Kong flats—so named be-cause they featured corn whiskey reputed to be as strong as King Kong. All these flats specialized in down-home "vittles"—deli-cacies like hog maws, chitterlings, cornbread, and skillet biscuits —all of which Teagarden craved and could not find outside Harlem.

Sallie Mae's pad in the basement on 133rd Street was the set-ting for an event that was unusual because Jack and Jimmy had great respect for each other's abilities. However, under the influ-ence of King Kong, fried chicken, and good fellowship, they squared away and blew, solo for solo, chorus for chorus, accompanied at first by Clarence Holiday's guitar and John Kirby's bass. When the news spread (as it always did), Sallie Mae's joint became crowded with tooters, and Cliff Jackson took over the comping on piano, along with George Stafford beating out rhythm on an old suitcase.

Actually, this confrontation was more of a friendly demonstration between, as we used to say, "the true bosses with the hot sauce," on how to extract the most swinging sounds out of the trombone than it was a real cutting session. Harrison gave new life to that old broad *Dinah*, while Teagarden had the cats screaming their approval when he swung—and I mean swung—in waltz time, *The World Is Waiting for the Sunrise!*

Sometimes the cutting sessions were less fraternal and more competitive. When Coleman Hawkins returned to his Harlem stomping grounds in 1939, after several years' absence in Europe, he was more than mildly concerned about whether the cats had caught up with him, as he put it. At that time, all the hippies hung out in former drummer Nightsie Johnson's joint, which I recall as on 131st Street near Saint Nicholas Avenue. Sunrise usually found the place filled with the cream of the entertainment world: musicians, singers, comics, dancers—Billy Daniels, Artie Shaw, and just about anyone else you could think of, but chiefly Billie Holiday, who, by her presence there every night, actually gave the impression that she owned the after-hours spot.

This was the setting for another of the most memorable cutting sessions. Hawk fell in about 3:00 or 4:00 A.M. without his instrument and just sat and sipped, listening until the last toot was tooted. All the cats paraded their wares before him because he was the big man—Hawkins had become king of the tenor saxes when he recorded *One Hour* and *Hello, Lola* with the Mound City Blue Blowers in 1929. They vied for his attention just in case he planned to start a band or had a record date on the fire—that was the talk among the assorted horn players: trumpets, trombones, and alto saxes.

But the tenor saxophonists had other ideas; they wanted to gain prestige by outplaying the master. They reasoned that

Coleman had been away from the source too long to know the hot licks that Harlem was putting down now. But what they'd forgotten was that Bean was a creative source within himself, an innovator rather than a copier. And I guess that most of the men were simply too young to realize how much of an old fox Coleman Hawkins was.

In any case, Hawk frequented the pad nightly for several weeks, and every time he was asked to play, he'd have another new excuse—he was resting from the constant grind of appearances in Europe, his horn was in pawn, he had a toothache, or he just couldn't bring himself to play in front of all these tenor giants. Fellows like Lester Young, Don Byas, Dick Wilson, Chu Berry, and many lesser talents were all itching to get a piece of the Hawk—especially Lester, whose staunchest fan was Billie Holiday.

One night Billie brought the personal element into focus by "signifying," which in Harlemese means making a series of pointed but oblique remarks apparently addressed to no one in particular, but unmistakable in intention in such a close-knit circle.

When Hawk ignored her, she proceeded to bring her opinions out into the open, saying that *her* man (and I figured at that time that she meant "her man" in more than one sense*) was the only tenor saxophone in the world, the one and only Pres, Lester Young, and it really wasn't any use for any tired old man to try and blow against her President.

Hawk took Lady Day's caustic remarks as a big joke, but apparently he'd previously decided that this was the night to make his move. Up to the last minute, the old fox played it cool, waiting until Billie's juice told her it was time for her to sing some blues. Then, he slipped out, returning with his saxophone, and started to accompany Billie's blues, softly. Billie, hearing his sound, looked up, startled and then motioned to Pres as if to say, "Take charge."

*According to several associates, and Lester Young himself, Rex—and others who figured the same—figured wrong. [Ed.]

So Lester began blowing the blues, and to give credit where credit is due, he really *played* the blues that night, chorus after chorus, until finally Hawk burst in on the end of one of his choruses, cascading a harmonic interruption, not unlike Mount Vesuvius erupting, virtually overpowering Lester's more haunting approach. When Hawk finished off the blues, soaring, searing, and lifting the entire house with his guttural, positive sonority, every tub began cheering, with the exception of Lady Day, Lester, and her pet boxer, Mister. They, like the Arabs, folded their tents and stole away.

Down Beat, March 7, 1967

Flow Gently, Sweet Rhythm
(John Kirby)

CREATIVITY, THAT INTANGIBLE QUALITY, sometimes bursts into flower out of the basic intelligence and ambitious drive of a have-not. Then fulfillment is achieved from the ashes of despair. Such was the remarkable story of John Kirby, who entered the world a discard, a foundling abandoned in the street.

Not the least of Kirby's problems was the dubious distinction of being born in 1908 in Baltimore, Maryland, then a city that refused to believe the South had lost the Civil War or that a person of color should be considered as anything other than chattel. John, who was too light to be colored and too colored to be white, caused considerable confusion among the authorities. Finally it was decided to place him in the Negro orphanage.

In later years, when John related his story to me, he declared the orphan home was hell and he could hardly wait until he was old enough to cope with the outside world. When the time came, he left and, following the customary adolescent pattern of those days, supported himself by selling newspapers, shining shoes, and grooming horses at the racetrack.

As he grew older, he realized that Baltimore was no place for him or any Negro, so he wangled a job as a Pullman porter on the Pennsylvania Railroad. That was his work until he joined Fletcher Henderson's orchestra.

On thinking about Kirby, I've often wondered why he never

mentioned any early musical background. Where, why, and how he got started playing tuba remains a mystery to me.

When he arrived in New York City, the big-town ways were a bigger mystery to him, because he was green and naive. To us would-be sophisticates in Smack's band, John's innumerable questions about every and any thing were at first a big joke, especially when he'd ask some question like what time could you catch the subway or why did some drugstores remain open all night. On looking back, I can appreciate his curiosity as an indication of the alert mind he later proved to have.

In his early New York days, John was a lonely person, and this stood out vividly as, one by one, he tried to ingratiate himself with us, without much luck, until he finally reached trombonist Jimmy Harrison. The way this came about bears retelling.

During that period, Smack's band was crazy with gambling fever, and our favorite game was blackjack, which we played for high stakes, betting five or ten dollars a hand. That kind of money was completely out of John's league, so we wouldn't let him play in our game. He'd stand around and kibitz, making everyone miserable with his coughing, giggling, and generally off-the-wall behavior. It was especially annoying when one of us lost a large bet. In desperation, Clarence Holiday, our guitarist, one night shouted, in effect, "Oh, let the bastard play. Maybe that will keep his mouth shut."

In any case, Kirby got into the game and within minutes had lost a week's salary. Jimmy felt sorry for him, and from then on, John became Jimmy's henchman. In effect, there was a threesome, for, at the time, Jimmy and Coleman Hawkins were inseparable. Kirby was in seventh heaven, hanging out with the big shots and aping their talk and telling their jokes. In his mind he also was a wheel.

In personality, John was quite different from June Coles, his predecessor in the bass department. June was a worldly, jovial, con-man type, at home under any circumstance, while John was a lonely, bewildered kid, who tried hard to be accepted by his peers. He finally succeeded because of his hail-fellow-well-met act, but when he was caught off guard, it was plain to see that Kirby really was introspective and a thinker.

Fate had dealt John a bollixed-up hand. The early years in the orphanage had left him without social graces, and he lacked formal education. He learned to cover up, but the hidden person emerged when he was in his cups. Moreover, his external appearance was nine-tenths Caucasian. But up in New York, ability counted, not color—quite the opposite from his hometown experience. As the crow flies, the distance from Baltimore to New York City is only about 190 miles, but the environmental and sociological barriers that Kirby had to overcome before making his mark as a musician, a bandleader, a creative force in jazz made New York seem a world away.

My first glimpse of Kirby still sticks in my mind. It happened while I was playing in the Roseland Ballroom with Fletcher. We were just getting onto the bandstand when a fellow who looked like an ofay from a distance furtively stumbled across the dance floor, loaded down with a big suitcase and a helicon tuba, the wrap-around type. What made his appearance so comical was the long green overcoat and the cap he was wearing. John's getup caused the fellows to snicker.

At first, we thought he was some kind of nut who had wandered into the place by mistake. As he drew closer, we could tell that he was not white. All eyes were on Kirby when we heard him say to Smack, "Well, here I am, Mr. Henderson. Where do I sit?" We were all amazed, because Smack had never mentioned a replacement for Coles, whom we were expecting—late as usual. The combination of our surprise and Kirby's manner broke us up, and for several seconds there was pandemonium on the bandstand as we rocked in uncontrollable gales of laughter. John just looked at us as if we were crazy, not quite realizing that he had caused the outburst.

I don't recall ever knowing where Henderson and Kirby met or how he happened to hire him, since there were many superior bass players around town. But it did not take long for John to learn the book. Of course, playing in the band and hanging out with us established cats after the gig was another matter. The pecking order was maintained, and most of the guys avoided Kirby.

However, gradually after a few months with Fletcher, the butterfly began to emerge from the cocoon. There were signs that, for all of his gaucheness and unworldliness, Kirby was no dummy. This realization came to the guys only slowly. At the time he joined the band everyone was too busy with his own affairs to pay much attention to Country Boy, as we nicknamed him.

There was the night John barged into the dressing room at Roseland, resplendent in a new overcoat, plus a pearl-gray homburg. We couldn't believe our eyes, and the questions outraced the exclamation of approval. John did not deign to answer any of us, although later, on the bandstand, he told Coleman Hawkins that he'd met some chick who had bought him the wardrobe. The truth came out later when we returned uptown and heard that Kirby had broken up a crap game, winning several hundred dollars—and blown it on the new togs.

An amusing episode involving John occurred when Wellman Braud, with Duke Ellington at the time, lent Kirby a bass fiddle. I suppose this was during the period when John was taking bass lessons from Braud. After John discontinued the lessons, he promised to return the instrument, but months passed, with Kirby making excuses and generally evading Braud.

When the inevitable confrontation took place, it was a beautiful spring afternoon. Crowding the sidewalks from the Rhythm Club to Seventh Avenue was a gang of musicians blocking traffic. Braud was observed turning the corner, togged out like an English toff, immaculate from head to foot and carrying his customary gold-headed cane. He smilingly entered the Rhythm Club after saying hello to various buddies, including me. I don't suppose he was there more than two minutes before Kirby burst out the door with Braud in pursuit. Kirby spun around the corner and was heading south on Seventh Avenue when Braud's cane connected with his noggin. Then it was all over. Kirby was sitting on the sidewalk, looking up at Wellman, and saying in a pleading voice,

"Let's quit this foolishness and talk it over." Braud agreed. All of the cats went wild with laughter.

On another occasion, John proved himself to be quite resourceful. The Henderson band was scheduled to play a dance in a Virginia tidewater town. As soon as we hit the burg, we noticed that there were no colored people flocking around our bus, which was strange, because usually when we arrived, it was like the circus coming to town. This time, however, what few folks we saw swept past us in a big hurry.

During the dance, we missed the customary hospitality. Although the dancers seemed to enjoy themselves, they made no requests and ignored the orchestra. One unpleasant thing I remembered was the attitude of the town policeman. During intermission, we headed for the men's room, but he barred the door, snarling, "ya-all cain't go in there. If ya gotta go, gwan out in the bushes."

The payoff, in which Kirby figured, came after the dance. We tried to buy gasoline for our bus only to find that our money was not acceptable. John spotted a five-gallon can, slipped out of the bus, and walked boldly into the station, seeming to have come from down the road. In real down-home accents, he demanded gas for his stalled car. The attendant took care of him at once, explaining that he only pumped gas for white folks and added that they'd lynched an uppity Negro two nights before. We drove down the road a bit, picked up John, and had a good laugh at Kirby's outwitting prejudice. Later, when we realized how close we had been to a dangerous situation, the laughter died down and turned into admiration for John.

After I had been fired from Smack's band for the last time, I did not see much of John because I'd gotten too involved with my own band at the Empire Ballroom on Broadway. Meanwhile, Kirby also had left Henderson and played with the little fellow who led the big band at the Savoy Ballroom, Chick Webb. It was with Chick that he really blossomed out and became an important bass player on the New York scene, recording many dates with artists like Mildred Bailey, the Andrews sisters, and Billie Holiday.

Perhaps it was during this period that he succumbed to that fatal disease that so many musicians contract—leaderitis.

When I heard that Kirby was rehearsing a combo with Pete Brown and Frankie Newton, I couldn't believe it. To me, Kirby just did not seem anything like leader material. However, time proved how wrong I was. He forged ahead to become one of the biggest leaders of any combo in the business. The time apparently was ripe for something new in jazz, and Kirby's highly arranged, tightly knit group had a very original sound.

As a rule, any organization worthy of the name is the result of the pooling of ideas. A group with sufficient talent and also the intelligence to understand that together they are a strong, composite voice, able to project and communicate as an entity, frequently attains greatness. (Lots of musicians never do realize this.) Kirby was lucky because he had all these things going for him.

Let's pause and reflect on the caliber of musicianship in the group that brought him fame. Charlie Shavers, one of the most underrated trumpet players in the business (then and now), was all of twenty when he joined Kirby, replacing another tremendous talent, that of Frankie Newton. Charlie, full of fire and creativity, and possessing extraordinary arranging ability, was the quarterback and sparkplug who provided, in his imaginative scores, the proper backgrounds and platforms to display the talents of pianist Billie Kyle, alto saxophonist Russell Procope, and clarinetist Buster Bailey, plus the tasteful vocals and drumming of O'Neil Spencer, whose excellent timekeeping kept them all on the ball.

John, in any other setting, probably would not have been chosen as the lad most likely to succeed. To the amazement of all who knew the man, Kirby's star as a bandleader began its ascendency. As a bandleader at the famed Café Society, a free-wheeling night club downtown, he was provided with the correct atmosphere to catapult the group into places that had had little or no swing music before—establishments like the Pump Room in Chicago, the Wedgewood Room in the Waldorf-Astoria Hotel in New York, and other such plush saloons all over the country.

Once the show was on the road, recording companies vied to get Kirby's name on a contract. Fan clubs sprang up. But he remained the same fellow from Baltimore. Although he'd become a big man, he still managed to give the appearance of an absent-minded professor staring at the world through rose-colored glasses.

Speaking of being absent-minded, the boys still enjoy relating Kirby's consternation when he arrived at a swanky club for an engagement, impeccable in his homburg, white scarf, and tuxedo, the total effect flawed only by his having on one black shoe and one brown.

Although musicians in general and the public adored the Kirby group, the jazz critics did not care for his excellent and tasteful brand of music. The know-it-alls of the late thirties and early forties felt that Kirby's approach was too stylized and overarranged, and this probably accounts for the regrettable lack of available commentary on his group.

As for John, he just laughed all the way to the bank. The jazz-band game is just about as uncertain as a horse race, but every now and then all the parts of the puzzle fall into place if one is lucky and also has an organization worthy of the chance. Lucky John at that time could have fallen into a sewer and found a diamond ring—and his fine group was eager to be heard.

Actually, Kirby's was not the first such group with this format. Kenneth Rhone, of Hartford, Connecticut, had formed a six-piece group in New York some years previously. Rhone, a trumpet player (and now an officer in Local 802) amazed Harlem with his avant-garde swinging and tight-knit arrangements. This excellent ensemble was unquestionably the forerunner of the Kirby approach and seemed to have a lot going for it, because all of the men doubled on instruments. This allowed a change of coloration that Kirby's group did not have. However, the element of luck must be considered, because Rhone didn't make it, and Kirby did.

The popularity of the Kirby records and the prestige of his theater and hotel dates opened still another door, and he was able to enter the even more lucrative field of radio. In 1940, Kirby's was the first Negro combo to be signed by a network (CBS), and it got a two-year contract for its own show—*Flow Gently, Sweet Rhythm.* The group also was heard on *Duffy's Tavern,* a popular program of the forties.

His own show also featured a popular vocalist of the time, the extremely talented Maxine Sullivan. John and Maxine were married for several years, but the marriage ended in divorce. John's second wife, Margaret, married to him until his death, was very helpful in providing me with material for this article.

John's fame grew until the war years cast a blight, not only on him but also the entire band business. The decline in his fortunes began when his anchor man, pianist Kyle, was drafted. Kirby never recovered from this blow nor did he ever really replace drummer Spencer. Gradually, the odds changed, and every day became more dismal, as personnel problems, travel restrictions, and dubious bookings took their toll. Finally, Kirby gave up and resigned himself to poring over his scrapbooks, dreaming out loud of departed glory.

While he was in his heyday, John always encouraged others in the profession to take a chance. For example, the late Canada Lee, the noted actor, almost refused his memorable role as Daniel DeBosola in the 1946 Broadway production of *The Duchess of Malfi* because the part called for him to appear made up as a Caucasian. Kirby harangued Lee until he accepted the challenge and starred so brilliantly that he was summoned to Hollywood to appear in movies. Also, it is not generally known that it was Kirby who played a significant role in convincing Lena Horne that she should accept her initial Hollywood offer. I am indebted to the late Buster Bailey for pointing out this facet of the Kirby personality.

Buster reminded me, too, about the days when he, John, and I were all members of the Fletcher Henderson Band. It may not be common knowledge that this band was one of the first, if not the first, eastern orchestra to make extensive road tours.

Touring was really a hassel those days and perhaps our biggest problem was the unavailability of food in the small burgs we played. This situation stemmed from the twin factors of discrimination and early closing hours in the smaller towns. So when there was food to be had, we ate to make up for lost meals, which resulted in the Henderson band gaining a reputation for eating like a passel of hungry alligators. Kirby, being impressionable, fell into the pattern and tried to outeat everyone, especially when it came to the sweet stuff like pies and cakes. I remember the time he bought a dozen charlotte russes and devoured them at one sitting.

His craving for sweets over the years probably aggravated the diabetes to which he succumbed in Los Angeles in 1952. After the decline of "The Biggest Little Band in the Land" and despite being warned by physicians that Scotch and insulin were not compatible, John chose that way out.

Down Beat, June 15, 1967

My Man, Big Sid
(Sidney Catlett)

O NE AFTERNOON, while en route to the Rhythm Club, I paused at the corner of 132nd Street and Seventh Avenue when I saw the sage of the Harlem musicians engaged in serious discussion with a fellow who was a stranger to me. The sage was Chick Webb, the alert, gregarious little drummer from Baltimore. The stranger loomed like a mountain over Chick, who was asking the fellow questions (as he usually did with everyone), and at the time, I supposed that he was merely passing the time of day with some truck driver fresh out of Bam (as Manhattanites called all the area south of New York's South Ferry).

As I drew closer, I was surprised to gather from their conversation that the big man was a musician. "Probably a bass player," I thought to myself, but having a date to play pool at the Club, I forgot about the stranger until a few days later. Then, somebody mentioned that Sammy Stewart had brought a good outfit in from Chicago and that the drummer was great. I didn't connect this with the man I'd seen until I fell into Small's Paradise one morning and found a drummers' session in full swing.

I don't remember everyone who was there, but I recall seeing Walter Johnson; Manzie Johnson; Nightsie Johnson; George Stafford, drummer for Charlie Johnson, who had the house band (and, incidentally, none of these Johnsons was related); Chick Webb; Kaiser Marshall from Fletcher Henderson's band; and Kid

Lips Hackette. It seemed as if every drummer in Harlem was there, standing around eying the stranger, Sid Catlett.

As daylight broke, Catlett not only proved to have as fast and skilled hands as anyone around town, but he also took one of his rare solos (Catlett didn't really like to solo). I suppose he sensed that this was his debut in the Big City, so he performed like a champ—not the usual drum gymnastics coming on like thunder, either. On the contrary, Sid gassed the house by taking a medium, relaxed tempo and working his snare and bass drum in conjunction, as if they were kissing cousins. Then he topped off the sequence by doing a stick-bouncing and stick-twirling spectacle that caused the entire house to burst into applause.

Such an artful exhibition delighted and bedazzled the audience, including me, despite my having witnessed several drummers doing the stick-bouncing and twirling tricks previously. However, Catlett's performance was the epitome of grace and beauty. Beads of sweat coursed down his mahogany-colored jaws as he chomped chewing gum in perfect rhythm with his drum beat.

As I watched, completely absorbed, I was quite aware that what Big Sid was doing was not unique, but the ease with which he recovered a far-flung stick or the comic twist he projected with a glance toward a cymbal—as though it were a naughty boy over which he had no control—was sheer genius.

Actually, such stick performances went way back to Buddy Gilmore, the drummer who starred with Will Marion Cook in 1919. I also had watched Rastus Crump, another sterling old-timer, feature this sort of technique with, as I recall, Gonzella White, who had a revue on the Columbia burlesque wheel. Count Basie later left the East Coast to go on the road with this group. Basie's cousin, Sonny Greer, was another great exponent of drum stickery. He created a sensation when he hit Washington, D.C., with this crowd-pleasing effect.

Today's tub-thumpers perhaps would frown on such a simple method of communication with drums, since they are so busy creating a self-image and playing melody on drums, of all things. No doubt, I am a fuddy-duddy, but I regret that most of the current crop never had the pleasure of hearing Big Sid and what he was putting down. In that context I must mention Kid Lips Hackette, who might be considered Big Sid's alter ego. While Hackette never hit the big time, and only played with territorial bands, like those of Frank Terry, Chick Carter, and Zack White, and although he did not resemble Catlett physically, he played very much like Sid and also did the drumstick solo in just about the same fashion, without missing a beat.

Big Sid was never ruffled, always alert, with a quick mind and perfect co-ordination. These qualities made him very popular with all the theatrical acts from Bill (Bojangles) Robinson down to dance teams like Tip, Tap, and Toe and Buck and Bubbles, as well as with chorus girls.

Aside from his talent, Sid was a big fellow in many ways. He was so big in heart that he made others, whose standing in the profession was more exalted, seem small by comparison. His generosity matched his size—a brawny six feet two inches—because he would give you the shirt off his back if you needed it. Usually relaxed and courteous, there still were occasions when the broad grin that customarily adorned his face would disappear, and a roar of anger would serve as a warning of impending violence— and the offender had better watch out!

Catlett was born in Evansville, Indiana, on January 17, 1910. He told me years later, jokingly, that his parents were concerned about his tiny size at birth but that the doctor reassured the anxious parents that the seven pound child would become a big fellow. These words were prophetic as little Sidney Catlett grew until he outgrew the town of Evansville and went on to Chicago.

There he acquired the nickname of Big Sid. By this time, he also had begun to acquire some reputation as a drummer—nothing spectacular, but the portents all pointed toward greatness. This embryo giant started his move, happily stretching his huge limbs, practicing drums, listening, watching, and learning.

Though he would slip away from home to venture into some joint on Chicago's south side, where perhaps Jasper Taylor or Baby Dodds was playing, he was always careful to get home before daybreak. As he later explained to me, he didn't want to worry his mother. But there did come a time when he begged, pleaded, and nagged her until she reluctantly gave Sid permission to leave home to become a professional drummer. There was one stipulation—he must return home from wherever he might be at Christmastime and spend the holidays with her. As far as I know, this promise was sacred to Catlett, because he always headed home at Christmastime. In any case, however, once he had his mother's consent, Big Sid put Chicago behind him.

I calculate that Sidney must have been probably sixteen when he started out in the profession and had about four years of seasoning around Chicago before he arrived in New York with Sammy Stewart. That would make Catlett about twenty years old at the time I met him, in 1930.

As a youngster, Sid loved all sports, but he was most partial to swimming. Together, in our youth, we used to frequent the Lido pool, which was located on Seventh Avenue at about 148th Street. Lots of the musicians went in for a swim, and most of the time one could find Louis Armstrong, Buster Bailey, John Kirby, Chu Berry, Don Redman, and sometimes Fats Waller among the throng who were on the spacious veranda where cooling potables were served. The popular drinks were mint juleps, Singapore slings, and Harlem's favorite, "top 'n bottom," which was a concoction of gin and port wine, which would make you high quickly and cheaply.

Although we were not working together in the same band at the time, Sid, tenor saxophonist Ben Webster, and I, for some unknown reason, used to find ourselves always together at the pool. We started calling each other by number. "Hey, Number One"— that would be Sid. Number Two was Ben, and I was Number Three. In the hubbub that accompanied the antics of more than 100 musicians and show people, this proved very effective, since each of us was able to whistle loudly through his fingers. One loud whistle signaled to Sid, and three whistles always alerted me to look for my buddies. Another thing that held us together might have been Ben's car. He had a new Buick and could always be counted on to drop Sid and me off at our homes after a swim.

When Catlett arrived in New York City, several of us musi-

cians had just finished roller skating as a pastime, and everybody
had gone in for bicycle riding. I remember how drummer George
Stafford had all of the cats drooling when he bought an English
bike. Assembling for our customary morning outing in front of
Small's Paradise one early June day, we were all surprised when
Big Sid spurted around the corner, coattails flying and all grins.
Up until then, he had not joined the bike riders. But there he was
in all his glory with his new bicycle. True, it was not a British
Sportster complete with gear shift, but we could tell it was a
premium wheel, and Sid was proud of it.

The setting was too perfect to avoid the good-natured rivalry
that existed in those days. Here were two of Harlem's top drummers, one a veteran and the other a newcomer, so the air was
charged with excitement as Stafford said to Catlett, "That's a
pretty machine you've got there, Sid. How about a race around
the block? Let's see which bike is the fastest."

They agreed to race three times around the block and the loser
was to buy drinks for the gang. They started off, and George was
leading all of the way until the very last time around when he
made the mistake of turning his head to wave at the bunch and
ran smack into a laundry truck. Luckily for him, the bundles of
clothes absorbed the shock, and no bones were broken. But Sid
won the race.

Later, Sid told us that he really didn't want to race George, because the difference in ages amounted to a handicap in his favor,
even though George's bicycle had gears and his did not.

Another sport that the Big Three—Stewart, Webster, and Catlett—liked to fool around with was basketball. Bob Douglas, who
operated the Renaissance Casino (which at the time was the home
of the famous Renaissance semipro basketball team), knew and
liked us. Often, we'd go up there in the afternoon and work out,
mostly throwing balls into the basket. This was fun, and all went
well for a while. Then Ralph Cooper, a popular emcee at the
Apollo Theater and a pretty good amateur athlete, decided to pit
his team of performers and musicians against the Renny team for
a benefit performance.

Naturally, being great tavern talkers, the Big Three announced they were going to play on the Cooper team. We all bought shoes and went into training, cutting down on our smoking and limiting our drinking to getting only half-loaded at night. I must say that Cooper was a good coach. He made Sid the center and Ben the left guard. But with me there was a problem in fitting me into the proper spot, and I wound up as the official water boy.

The big night arrived, and the Casino was crowded. Cheers greeted each announced name, even mine. It was no contest, of course, although I had that water bucket swinging. Webster managed to steal the ball once from the pros, and Sid really starred. He sank a basket, scoring for our team, and was going great guns until somebody accidentally stepped on his foot. Then, the air turned blue, as Sid limped off the court cursing and yelling, "They fouled me!"

It was not too long after the basketball fiasco that I became afflicted with leaderitis and put together a big band of thirteen pieces for a Broadway ballroom, the Empire. The band was distinguished by the fact that all the saxophones doubled violin. The thirteenth man was Sonny Woods, whom I had brought into New York from Pittsburgh to do the vocals (later, he was featured with Louis Armstrong's big band). My drummer? Big Sid Catlett, of course, a fact that has escaped some historians.

The year was 1931, the depth of the depression, which worked to my advantage, since I was able to assemble a talented bunch of musicians. Sid sparked the band and was the number one crowd-pleaser. On the occasion of our first radio broadcast, he really saved our necks. I was supposed to give the downbeat for the theme but froze with nervousness. Sid came in with a rhythmic succession of beats, which filled the gap until I recovered my wits.

Sidney's tenure with us ended when Christmastime came around, as, much to everyone's dismay, he cut out for Chicago and his mother. While he was in the Windy City, we lost the gig. Still, we had had a thirteen-month engagement after originally being booked for only two weeks. While the band broke up a couple of months later, Catlett went on to greater heights. Paramount among his gifts was his sense of fitness in a group large or small, which projected Sid into the limelight. He inuititively chose a particular rhythmic pattern or beat that enhanced the soloist of the moment.

On the East Coast, during the thirties and forties, there was a group of four colored theaters (the Howard in Washington, the Royal in Baltimore, the Pearl in Philadelphia, and the Apollo in New York City) left over from the ancient Theater Owners Booking Association (TOBA) chain. These houses were called "the round the world circuit" by show people, including musicians, which is one indication of how low the business had sunk for the profession (the Harlem members, that is).

Each house maintained a resident chorus line of fifteen or so girls, with the girls vying for the reputation of constituting the greatest dancing line. The chorus girls' jobs really depended on how well their dance routines went over with the audiences, and this resulted in the drummer's being the key figure. If he was not adept and quick to accompany those intricate dance steps, the routine would bomb, and the girls would start cursing the drummer and the band.

Catlett's ability to catch the dancers' steps and emphasize every tap just as they performed them made him the favorite of all of the chorus girls. Ristina Banks' best chorus soon discovered Sid's talent, and that was important, because she had the group at the Apollo in New York. To her, there was no drummer like Sid.

Bandleaders who were fortunate enough to have Sid in their orchestras agreed. He was the number one drummer wherever he went, and he played in a variety of bands. Personally, I remember his playing with Sammy Stewart, Benny Carter, McKinney's Cotton Pickers, Jeter-Pillars in Saint Louis, Fletcher Henderson, Don Redman, Benny Goodman, Louis Armstrong, and Teddy Wilson, in addition to the stint with my band. There must be some groups that I have overlooked, but any way you figure it, that's a lot of bands to have played with.

In 1947 I went to Europe and didn't see Sid again until I returned in 1950. Taking a hiatus from playing, I bought a farm but soon found that this was a money-losing proposition. So I packed my horn and retreated to New York. After devoting a few evenings to looking up old cronies and trying to extract a possible job lead, I ran into Sid. We got to talking about the state of the business. We thought that things were tough then (in 1950), but little did we know that it was going to get tougher.

Sid was in a good position, as far as I could see, because he could play with the swing groups as well as the bop groups. However, Sid was feeling uneasy, and we spoke about the evils existing in the business, agreeing on every point.

Right then we decided to get together an all-star band. I am sure that the idea sprang from Sid's telling me that one of the biggest bookers had assured him of steady bookings if he put together a good group. This we proceeded to do, with Ken Kersey, piano; Benny Morton, trombone; Buster Bailey, clarinet; Lloyd Trottman, bass; myself, cornet; and Catlett, drums.

After a bit of woodshedding to set the routines, we opened at the Hurricane at Forty-ninth and Broadway, and I led the group. We had a two-week engagement there, followed by a week at the Showboat in Philly. Then, we got a week in Boston, playing the Hi-Hat Club. By that time, the handwriting was on the wall.

Buster Bailey left and was replaced by Edmond Hall. Sid and I were becoming disenchanted, since we had promoted the gigs ourselves, and, after we closed Boston, Catlett started haunting Mr. Big's anteroom, hoping he would keep his promise about booking Sid's group. But he was never "in." Then, I got the idea of sending him telegrams (in Sid's name), and still nothing happened. So after a month, I returned to my farm, saying good-bye to the fellows.

It was then late fall, and I suppose that Sid went home to mom in Chicago for his usual Christmas visit. He never came back. Big Sid, only forty-one years old, had a heart attack after the holidays and died early in 1951. If he were still around, he could show some of these modern drummers a thing or two about communication, both with his fellow musicians and the audience.

Fortunately, Sid did a lot of recording, and his easy style lives on, to be heard, studied, or just enjoyed by a new generation who have lost the opportunity to evaluate this great man in person. For my money, Sid Catlett was the greatest.

Down Beat, November 17, 1966

The Benny Carter I Knew

FREQUENTLY RECOGNIZED jazz musicians of years' standing have had considerable coverage in publications during their lifetime, even though the publications may not be of huge national circulation. However, a rave review in a trade magazine or a brief accolade in a newspaper column does not give a nearly satisfying or complete picture of the individual as a human being—his motivations, character, or environmental influences. With such depth reporting growing more and more important to the world of the scholar, to the jazz buff, to posterity, and to me personally, I invite you to a word portrait of Bennett Lester Carter.

Carter's countenance is deceptively mild. His ready wit, smile, his soft, quick speech also give slight indication of the iron will encased in his brilliant mind. Of imposing stature, he moves with the poise and grace of those accustomed to walking with kings. Perhaps that explains why those who know him best call him "king."

Carter is an affable, courtly gentleman. His gentility almost seems to be out of a forgotten age. This is not to imply that Benny is in any way a placid person—quite the contrary. When the occasion merits, the warm brown eyes can change in a flash to a cold, darker, indescribable color that virtually shouts, "Look out!" This metamorphosis happens rarely, but when it does, everyone involved knows it.

I first met Benny about the first part of 1922, to the best of my recollection (he quibbles with me over the exact year but not the details). During that period, I was a disciple of Bubber Miley, the trumpet boss of Harlem. Bubber got carried away with some good right-off-the-boat whiskey one morning and, as a result, was unable to make the matinee at John O'Connor's club on 135th Street in New York City. Since neither Gus Allen nor Bobby Stark could be found, I got the job to play in Bubber's place.

As I walked in with my little cornet, I could see that O'Connor didn't particularly relish the substitution, but he didn't say anything to me. I sat down and started to play along with the guys. Let's see . . . in that band were trombonist Geechy Fields, T-Bone Spivvy on guitar, Fats Smitty on piano, Crip the drummer, and myself on cornet. Some kid was supposed to substitute for the sax man Ben Whitted, too, but hadn't shown up at starting time.

Ten minutes after we began to play, a fellow with a skinny body and a big head (at least his head seemed to belong to another body at that time) ambled across the dance floor, up to the bandstand, and unpacked a sax. We looked at each other, wondering who this was, what was the sax, and if this was Whitted's substitute. It turned out that this was the first time any of us had laid eyes on Benny. The saxophone was a C melody. And Whitted *had* sent him.

I guess that two ringers replacing his regular bandsmen was just too much for the boss, especially since they didn't cut the mustard too well. After two numbers, O'Connor called Benny over and handed him some handbills advertising the club, saying, "You'll do my place more good standing on the corner passing these out to the people than tooting on that hornpipe."

Rest in peace, John O'Connor, rest in peace. You couldn't have known how Benny would turn out. It's too bad you will never realize that you once sent one of the world's greatest saxophonists to the corner to pass out handbills.

That was my introduction to Benny Carter. I was not impressed. Neither were the other fellows, but fate must have got a large-size chuckle.

After that episode, I didn't see Carter for quite some time. I lived up in Harlem while he lived downtown in a neighborhood nicknamed "the jungle." I seldom ventured down there. It was the kind of section you had to be well known in. Otherwise it was better to stay away, unless you liked the idea of carrying your head in your hand as you exited on the run.

I didn't run into Benny again until about a year later when Happy Caldwell (a great and unheralded influence on tenor saxophone) talked me into going on a job in Asbury Park, New Jersey. I went because I trusted Caldwell's judgment—he was older and more experienced than I. We hied ourselves to the Park, seeking fame and fortune. There, we met Carter and Bobby Stark. But Happy and I got canned after the first week, and there followed my first real panic. I'd been stranded before—when our hometown band didn't get paid in Richmond, Virginia, and later in Philly with the ill-fated *Go-Get-It* show, but both of those times I had been part of a group, and there were lots of ways to console each other and share the misery.

This time it was different—it was Happy and Rex against the world. No buddies, no relatives, and no job. The panic didn't last too long because Happy knew his way around. We spent part of each day finding a sheltered place to sleep (on a pool table, in somebody's basement, etc.) and the rest of the time hustling hot-dog money. Sometimes we'd split one hot dog between us and then drink a tomato-juice cocktail, made of catsup and water. This was for free.

Stark and Carter joined us for a while when they also got the ax, but their situation was not the same as ours. They had gotten into a fracas, because Bobby drank so much the boss had to fire them, which resulted in their being told by the law to get out of town. That was a drag to them, as it was to us, since none of us wanted to return to New York in the dead of summer, a failure, after bragging that we were good enough to spend a whole season playing Asbury Park.

In the late twenties and early thirties, the times were right, and despite the throngs of musicians flocking to New York, there were still not enough skilled men to go around all of the clubs, dance halls, and joints. Most of these places were quite happy to have us blowing in them, because our jamming not only provided atmosphere and free music for the customers but also considerable revenue—the tooters were notorious spenders. It was real cozy for everybody, and we were never at a loss for a place to tab drinks, to experiment, let off steam, and enjoy ourselves with our fellows.

Mind you, we were also learning all of the time. One thing soon became clear to me: the best players were the best listeners. Jimmy Harrison, Coleman Hawkins, Tommy Dorsey, Bix Beiderbecke, Benny Carter, and numerous others all listened, and all of them later emerged as top performers in the profession. This supports my contention that a large part of genius lies not only in ability, comprehension, and imagination but also in the willingness to listen and learn—along with an innate sense of propriety. Carter possesses this combination of qualities to such a degree that his place among the masters is assured. Attaining that place, of course, took time.

When next I heard anything about him, we were playing in Newark, New Jersey, with a fellow named Bobby Brown, who had rescued both Happy and me from Asbury Park. Brown had a good group, was ambitious, and always traveled to New York to hear the latest in music and musicians. After one such jaunt, he returned raving about some guy who played with Charlie Johnson at Ed Small's new place called Small's Paradise. To hear Brown tell it, this alto sax man was the greatest since high-button shoes, and his name was Benny Carter! Happy looked at me, and I looked at Happy. We both thought the same thing. Is he kidding? We'd known Carter for some time, and he'd never baked beans for us, not real Boston style (in the early days, taking a solo chorus was termed "taking a Boston" and/or "getting off").

Anyway, Happy and I had our curiosity aroused, and on our night off, we visited Small's. I felt right at home, since I had not only worked for Ed at his Sugar Cane but also was on close terms with him, since I had roomed at his home on 137th Street. There was a small section right next to the bandstand where the musicians used to congregate and listen to the band without having to pay the usual tariff for drinks, which was great with us.

Johnson's band was in fine form and really rocking the joint. Everybody, that is, except Carter, who was leaning in his chair against the railing of the bandstand with his eyes closed. He didn't even see us at first. I remember turning my head to Happy and then hearing a cascade of notes in a brief alto saxophone solo that was unbelievable.

Sure enough, it was Benny Carter. Bobby Brown had not exaggerated a bit. Benny was truly outstanding, although it was hard to believe that he was in a musical climate that produced such stalwarts as Eugene Fields, Ben Whitted, Fess Edmonds—all formidable exponents of the alto for their time. There were also the great Carmelito Jejo, who played liked greased lightning, and among the younger lads there was competition from Harvey Boone, Lester Boone (no relation), Johnny Hodges, Charlie Holmes, Pete Brown, and Edgar Sampson. But Benny Carter was the boss!

That night, after we'd had our ears opened, George Stafford, the drummer, remarked, "Benny sure sleeps a lot on the stand, but he always comes in at the right places for his solos."

"I never saw anything like it," Johnson echoed.

Shortly thereafter, I saw Benny sleep a whole lot more when he and I both roomed in the apartment of Billy Taylor, the bass player. One day, Benny said, "I think I'll learn to arrange." Well, Taylor had been studying arranging a lot and had become discouraged. As for me, I was having so much trouble reading the music with Elmer Snowden that I felt Benny was just day-dreaming. He wasn't.

It was about two years later, after I had joined Fletcher Henderson. I usually stopped by Small's after I finished my night's stint at Roseland, and Benny, Billy, and I went home together. One night, business was slack at Small's, so the group was rehearsing a splendid arrangement of a popular tune of the day.

When they finished the rundown, I was amazed and delighted to learn that Benny had made the chart. What I couldn't figure out was when Benny had studied arranging. After all, we lived in the same apartment, and neither Taylor nor I was aware of his developing talent. In any case, that night up in Harlem, the torch was lit, the child was born. Carter had started on a long and illustrious career.

This gift smoldered for quite some time, with bright emissions through the bands of Fletcher Henderson, Chick Webb, McKinney's Cotton Pickers. But the real big time proved elusive until Benny was summoned by the British Broadcasting Company to become staff arranger in 1936. Leonard Feather, a perceptive observer and chronicler of the jazz scene, had passed on the word to the powers that be at the network that Benny Carter was the man for the position.

After three years at BBC, Benny returned home to the then healthy big-band field, in which he consolidated his position as a ranking peer. Already established as a better-than-average clarinetist (which he prefers not to acknowledge) and a consummate delineator of the beauties of the alto saxophone (he says that the late Frankie Trumbauer was his inspiration), Carter astonished everyone by playing a moving and articulate trumpet. Such talent would seem enough for two persons, but not for Bennett Lester Carter—he then demonstrated his virtuosity by playing piano and trombone too.

There are so many incidents regarding Benny that are etched in my memory. . .

In Taylor's apartment, my room was adjacent to Benny's. He would knock on the wall, "Stew, are you asleep?" If I answered, he'd continue: "What note is this?" Then he'd hit a high note on his horn or even whistle a tone. I'd speculate and answer what note I thought it was. Then he would play a devilish trick on me. By plotting with Taylor, they succeeded in convincing me that I was tone deaf. They always agreed with each other as to what note was being hit or played over a period of weeks. For instance, they'd call a concert D, E, and so forth. But I finally got wise when I started bringing my cornet home every night so that I could check.

Later, during the time Benny was leading the Horace Henderson Orchestra, he again got on a sound kick. Every sound had to be identified and related to its proper place on the scale. We were touring at this time and had ample opportunity to hear train whistles, fog horns, and even bull frogs croaking. Many times Benny would stop that big old Studebaker and have someone pull out a trumpet or clarinet to sound a note he would stipulate just to see if he had heard the tone of, say, a train whistle right.

The Henderson band headquartered at Wilberforce University in southern Ohio. One Sunday morning, we received a phone call telling us to open at a place called Blue Island Lake, thirty-five miles from Detroit and 225 miles from Wilberforce, as I recall, and we were to be there by Monday at 8:00 P.M. This took quite a bit of doing, since we had only two cars, one of which was the jalopy Benny owned at the time. Eleven of us, plus gear, had to be squeezed in.

Henry Hicks was driving a fairly new Chrysler with good tires, and Carter drove that big, old Studebaker touring sedan, with rubber bands and spit for tires. To make everything dandy, that year we were having an early fall, so it was unseasonably cool.

We left the Force early and had got only as far as Columbus when the first of many tire blowouts happened. After that, they occurred with such frequency that we started to make bets as to how far we would get before the next one. Oh, what fun to be young!

When we finally limped into Detroit at about 6:00 P.M. on Monday, we were plenty tired, dirty, and hungry, with still another forty miles to go to Blue Island Lake. We stoked up on food and booze, changed into clean shirts, and were on time, ready to blow like mad all night, which we did.

The climax of the trip came when we were happily trekking back to Detroit and bed. Rrrr. Sirens and flashing red lights appeared suddenly. Squads of police headed us into the curb, lined us up, searched the car, and questioned us for about half an hour.

It seemed like an eternity, tired as we were. When they let us go, they explained that a car just like ours had been identified as a getaway vehicle in a bank holdup earlier that night.

Benny and I, having played together in Fletcher's band, Horace's Wilberforce Collegians, and McKinney's Cotton Pickers, used to eat together most of the time, and we became famous as trenchermen almost everywhere we went. This is what happened in Cincinnati, at Uncle Henry's:

We would come in and give our usual chant: "Good bread, good meat, good God, let's eat." Uncle Henry shuddered as we thus blessed the bounteous table for the "wrecking crew," composed of Joebeatus McCord, Talcott Reeves, Henry Hicks, Benny, and me. As I look back to that table of Uncle Henry's, my taste buds water . . . mountains of mashed potatoes, platters of roast pork, fried chicken, flanked by corn on the cob, salad, hot rolls, hot biscuits, corn bread, and gravy. This kind of spread was an everyday affair with the gentleman, but to us ever-hungry bandsmen, it was a treat to play Cincinnati just so we could get the wrinkles out of our stomachs at Uncle Henry's. However, like all good things, it had to end somewhere, and after we had annihilated his table every day for a week, he finally said, "Sorry, fellows. I can't afford to feed you for fifty cents a meal. From now on, you will have to pay me double." Our pleas for leniency because of hardship fell on deaf ears.

Oh, we had fun in those days . . . talking music, playing together, rehearsing, living the life of the world as seen through the eyes of twenty-year-olds. Every town beckoned to come and enjoy its newness.

We thrived on playing practical jokes on each other. One they played on me I'll never forget. It happened on a Sunday morning and I had just fallen into bed like a ton of bricks. The next thing I knew, the bed started doing the rhumba, awakening me with a terrible start. My first thought was that we were having one of those rare earthquakes. But this was too violent. My next thought was that I had succumbed to delirium tremens, for I remembered hearing from other brothers that too much whiskey could bring them on. To my great relief, I discovered two ropes attached to the bottom of the bed, one leading to Billy Taylor's room and the other to that playful prankster, Benny Carter. We all found this so hilarious that we woke up the house with our laughter and almost got put out.

On the other side of the scale was Benny's strong sense of dignity when the occasion demanded. One such incident was the confrontation of Benny by Uncle Bo, as we called Bill (Bojangles) Robinson. Bojangles was quite a figure in the twenties and thirties. Creator of a unique style of tap dancing and a rather influential fellow in some circles, Uncle Bo was a capricious and sometimes good-hearted soul. His greatest flaw, perhaps, was his mouth, which, as I recall, he could never turn off. There would always be a lecture, whether the subject was baseball, women, gambling, the church, or whatever. Uncle Bo always had a lot to say, and most people humored him. If by some chance, they did not agree with his view, he enjoyed making a production out of flashing his gold-plated pistola to emphasize the point. The fact that the weapon came with a deputy sheriff's badge made Uncle Bo kind of cantankerous at times.

The time I remember was in a rehearsal hall next door to the old Lafayette Theater in Harlem. The cast of the next week's production was being shaped by the producer, Leonard Harper. Benny was leading the band for the show, and I was playing third trumpet. Rehearsing in one corner of the huge cavern of a hall, a trio of tap dancers was thundering through complex routines. In another corner, Ristina Banks, captain of the dancing chorus, was guiding and cajoling her girls through the dances. In a third corner, Tom Whaley, Harper's music director, sat at the piano coaching some females with their songs. The band was in the center of this pandemonium. It was 4:30 A.M., and everybody was dead tired. I was dozing and almost asleep, so I missed the start of what happened, but suddenly, the room grew quiet, and that woke me up in time to hear someone say, "Here comes Uncle Bo, looking like Faust! That's all we need this morning."

Whoever said that must have been a fortune teller with a real working crystal ball. Sure enough, Bojangles took over. First, he criticized the tap dancers, telling them that they were not to do a certain step without his permission, since he had invented it. They left after promising to take the step out of their act, and next came a demonstration for the chorus girls on how to make an exit. All this interference coming from Bojangles was not unusual. We knew that, despite his crude way of taking over, as a rule he meant well. But when I saw Benny Carter's left eye begin to twitch, I recognized it meant danger for somebody. The somebody was Bojangles Robinson.

Before going further, I should point out that Bojangles was not a bad fellow, and his egocentric compulsions doubtless resulted more from a significant lack of formal education in a self-made man than from any calculated mischief making. Adored as he was by the white audiences of his time, Robinson was pretty hard to take among his own people, especially the younger ones.

The tableau that unfolded proved a memorable one. There in a brief span of minutes, we witnessed the oldster slowly becoming aware that his day had waned and the baton had passed on to the younger folk.

The opening salvo started when Uncle Bo told Benny that the tempo of the production number was too slow. Benny didn't answer but gave Robinson a long hard stare. Producer Harper, anxious to continue his rehearsal, called out, "Okay, Benny, take down the opening. Places, everybody!" We shuffled through our music, Benny stomped off the tempo and then gave the downbeat. All of the guys seemed relieved and quite happy to be playing, tired as we were, feeling the sound of music would either appease or drown out the haranguing of Bojangles. But he had other ideas. We'd play only about eight bars when he rushed up to Carter shouting, "Oh *no!* Good God almighty, what kind of tempo do you call this? Stop 'em, stop this damn band. I'll give you the right time for this number." Benny never took the horn from his mouth, and the band kept playing as Uncle Bo grew more exasperated. After a few seconds, he grabbed Benny's arm, and that did it. The band stopped, the rehearsal fizzled like a wet firecracker. Dancers, chorus girls, and musicians suddenly had business somewhere else. In my time, I've heard some fine choices of the customary words employed in that type of encounter, but never have I seen the air turn blue and then pink, almost as if it were blushing.

The disagreement went on loud and long, culminating in a tussle in which Benny was forced to take Bojangles' gold-plated revolver away from him, to avoid being shot. Harlem buzzed for days over the news that a young musician had not only stood up to the mayor of Harlem (as Uncle Bo was known at that time) but had, by disarming him, humiliated and irretrievably damaged Bojangles' image.

Another incident concerning Carter comes to mind, but first I would like to explain and qualify any impression I may be creating of him as a brawler. Now, and for many years, he has been the antithesis of a rowdy person, though in his younger days there were times when exacerbated circumstances propelled him into action he probably would have as soon forgotten. Further, in an article of this sort—not, I hope, the usual glamorous treatment accorded great figures that leaves the reader feeling something is missing—I chose material I hope will present a rounded picture.

It was during a sabbatical leave of absence from Duke Ellington, in 1943, I think, that I happened to be in Los Angeles. Wanting to keep my chops in shape, I played several dates with Carter's band. This was, of course, previous to the decline of the big bands. The war was on, and this unforgettable experience took place in a San Diego club, where we were playing a dance.

The night was balmy, the girls were gay, the pride of our Navy was in the mood for frolic. Benny's band was a good one, as always, and this evening all the vibrations of the fellows were attuned to the music. They were cooking. Everything was groovy until one of the sailors, evidently carried away by the magic of the moment, yanked Benny's trouser leg as he danced by the shoulder-high bandstand and yelled, "Play *Stardust*, Sambo!"

Everybody on the bandstand who heard the remark shuddered. The band played on, as Benny nodded, acknowledging the sailor's request. However, apparently the lad didn't, or couldn't, get the message because after making a turn around the hall, he repeated his words and action. This was a mistake. Benny unhooked his alto, jumped off the stand, threw three punches to floor the big redhead, jumped back on the stand, picked up his horn, and resumed playing. The entire sequence took only about eight bars in a medium-bounce tempo. As his buddies poured water on the sailor and took him away, I was sorry about the whole episode; I always enjoyed playing Benny's arrangement of *Stardust*.

The years have been kind to Carter, and Carter's music has unquestionably been kind to the world's ears. Music like *Cow-Cow Boogie*, the late Freddie Slack's tour de force; *Blues in My Heart* (his first published effort); Peggy Lee's singing of his tune *Lonely Woman*; *The Caring Kind*, *Rainbow Rhapsody*, *When Lights Are Low*, *Blue Star* highlight his extensive catalog with ASCAP.

As a result of Benny's affinity for good comradeship and the social graces, his mail abounds with invitations, and his phone rings with others. Despite his heavy schedule, he still tries very hard to enjoy life away from the grind of work. Perhaps Benny's greatest regret is having to leave a party at its height. But "those schedules must be met," he'll smilingly yawn as he leaves.

Most fellow musicians know that he stays busy enough for two men, arranging music for this movie sequence or that television show (currently, he is involved with the Chrysler show). Sandwiched in between, he conducts and arranges record dates for Peggy Lee, Sarah Vaughan, Lou Rawls, Pearl Bailey—there are too many to mention.

A little-known fact about Carter is his consistent search for talent—but I hasten to advise young hopefuls: don't call him. He's too busy. But maybe if you are lucky, fate will beckon if your paths cross, as it did for both Felicia Saunders and Ruth Olay. Some twelve years ago, Benny took his band to San Diego for a month's booking and took the two then unknown vocalists along. Voila! The band clicked and the girls were launched on their talented careers.

The most valid record of a major musician's contributions are found on phonograph and tape machines. The great innovators are passing away—Jack Teagarden, Don Redman, Claude Thorn-hill—and many others remain only as memories. In the foreseeable future most of the vitality and beauty of this U.S. art form will be found only in other countries, in an adulterated form. It would be a great service to music and the United States if someone would commission Benny Carter to compose, arrange, and choose personnel for a recording of his music for posterity. Though he is composing, arranging, and recording now, he does not have free rein to write the music of his choice or to select the artists in many cases. It will be a pity if the world loses the opportunity to hear the entire spectrum of the talents of Benny Carter.

Down Beat, October 7, 1965

Genius in Retrospect
(Art Tatum)

A T EVERY DANCE that Fletcher Henderson's band played there'd be someone boasting about hometown talent. Usually, the local talent was pretty bad, and we were reluctant to take the word of anyone but a darn good musician, such as alto saxophonist Milton Senior of McKinney's Cotton Pickers, who was touting a piano player.

"Out of this world," Milton said. We were persuaded to go to the club where this pianist was working. The setting was not impressive; it was in an alley, in the middle of Toledo's Bohemian section. I'm not sure if the year was 1926 or '27, but I am sure that my first impression of Art Tatum was a lasting one. As a matter of fact, the experience was almost traumatic for me, and, for a brief spell afterward, I toyed with the idea of giving up my horn and returning to school.

Looking back, I can see why Tatum had this effect on me. Not only did he play all that piano, but, by doing so, he also reminded me of how inadequately I was filling Louis Armstrong's chair with the Henderson band.

To a man, we were astonished, gassed, and just couldn't believe our eyes and ears. How could this nearly blind young fellow extract so much beauty out of an old beat-up upright piano that looked like a relic from the Civil War? Our drummer, Kaiser Marshall, turned to Henderson and said it for all of us:

"Well, it just goes to show you can't judge a book by its cover. There's that beat-up old piano, and that kid makes it sound like a Steinway. Go ahead, Smack, let's see you sit down to that box. I bet it won't come out the same."

Fletcher just shrugged his shoulders and answered philosophically, "I am pretty sure that we are in the presence of one of the greatest talents that you or I will ever hear. So don't try to be funny."

Coleman Hawkins was so taken by Tatum's playing that he immediately started creating another style for himself, based on what he'd heard Tatum play that night—and forever after dropped his slap-tongue style.

To our surprise, this talented youngster was quite insecure and asked us humbly, "Do you think I can make it in the big city [meaning New York]?" We assured him that he would make it, that the entire world would be at his feet once he put Toledo behind him. Turning away, he sadly shook his head, saying, kind of to himself, "I ain't ready yet."

However, as far as we were concerned, he was half-past ready! I can see now that Tatum really thought he was too green and unequipped for the Apple, because he spent the next few years in another alley in another Ohio city—Cleveland—at a place called Val's.

It was probably at Val's that Paul Whiteman "discovered" him a year or so later, when Art was nineteen, and took him to New York to be featured with the Whiteman band. But insecurity and homesickness combined to make him miserable, and after a short time, he fled back to Toledo. This is a good example of a man being at the crossroads and taking the wrong turn.

After returning home, Tatum gradually became confident that he could hold his own. When Don Redman was passing through Toledo a year or so later, Art told him, "Tell them New York cats to look out. Here comes Tatum! And I mean every living 'tub' with the exception of Fats Waller and Willie the Lion."

At that time, Art had never heard of Donald (The Beetle) Lambert, a famous young piano player around New York in the twenties, and he came into the picture too late to have heard

Seminole, an American Indian guitar and piano player, whose left hand was actually faster than most pianists' right hands. In any case, to Tatum, Fats was Mr. Piano.

The admiration was reciprocated. The story goes that Fats, the cheerful little earful, was in great form while appearing in the Panther Room of the Sherman Hotel in Chicago. Fats was in orbit that night, slaying the crowd, singing, and wiggling his behind to his hit *Honeysuckle Rose*.

Suddenly, he jumped up like he'd been stung by a bee and, in one of those rapid changes of character for which he was famous, announced in stentorian tones: "Ladies and gentlemen, God is in the house tonight. May I introduce the one and only Art Tatum." I did not witness this scene, but so many people have related the incident that I am inclined to believe it.

At any rate, before Tatum did much playing in New York, he spent a period of time with vocalist Adelaide Hall as part of a two-piano team, the other accompanist being Joe Turner (the pianist). Miss Hall, then big in the profession, took them with her on a European tour.

In appearance, Tatum was not especially noteworthy. His was not a face that one would pick out of a crowd. He was about five feet seven inches tall and of average build when he was young but grew somewhat portly over the years. Art was not only a rather heavy drinker but was also fond of home cooking and savored good food. As he became affluent, his favorite restaurant was Mike Lyman's in Hollywood, which used to be one of Los Angeles' best.

An only child, Tatum was born in Toledo October 13, 1910. He came into the world with milk cataracts in both eyes, which impaired his sight to the point of almost total blindness. After thirteen operations, the doctors were able to restore a considerable amount of vision in one eye. Then Tatum had a great misfortune; he was assaulted by a holdup man, who, in the scuffle, hit Tatum in the good eye with a blackjack. The carefully restored vision was gone forever, and Tatum was left with the ability to see only large objects or smaller ones held very close to his "good" eye.

Art had several fancy stories to explain his blindness, and a favorite was to tell in great detail how a football injury caused his lack of sight. I've heard him go into the routine: he was playing halfback for his high school team on this rainy day; they were in the huddle; they lined up; the ball was snapped . . . wait a minute—there's a fumble! Tatum recovers . . . he's at the forty-five yard line, the thirty-five, the twenty-five! Sprinting like mad, he is heading for a touchdown! Then, out of nowhere, a mountain falls on him, and just before oblivion descends, Tatum realizes he has been tackled by Two-Ton Tony, the biggest fellow on either team. He is carried off the field, a hero, but has had trouble with his eyes ever since.

The real stories about Art are so unusual that one could drag out the cliché about fact being stranger than fiction. When Art was three, his mother took him along to choir practice. After they returned home, she went into the kitchen to prepare dinner and heard someone fumbling with a hymn on the piano. Assuming that a member of the church had dropped by and was waiting for her to come out of the kitchen, she called out, "Who's there?" No one answered, so she entered the parlor, and there sat three-year-old Art, absorbed in playing the hymn.

He continued playing piano by ear, and he could play anything he heard. Curiously, there was once a counterpart of Tatum in a slave known as Blind Tom. Tom earned a fortune for his master, performing before amazed audiences the most difficult music of his time after a single hearing. But Tom couldn't improvise; he lacked the added gift that was Tatum's.

Tatum played piano several years before starting any formal training. He learned to read notes in Braille. He would touch the Braille manuscript, play a few bars on the piano, touch the notation, play . . . until he completed a tune. After that, he never had to "read" the song again; he knew it forever. He could play any music he had ever heard. One time, at a recording session, the singer asked if he knew a certain tune. Art answered, "Hum a few bars." As the singer hummed, Art was no more than a half-second behind, playing the song with chords and embellishments as if he had always known it, instead of hearing it then for the first time.

His mother, recognizing that he had an unusual ear, gave him four years of formal training in the classics. Then, the day came when the teacher called a halt to the studies, saying, "That's as far as I can teach you. Now *you* teach *me*."

Tatum carried his perception to the nth degree. Eddie Beal, one of Art's devoted disciples, recalls their first meeting, which happened at the old Breakfast Club on Los Angeles' Central Avenue about 4:00 A.M. The news had spread that Tatum was in town and could be expected to make the scene that morning. Just as Tatum entered the room, as Beal tells it, "whoever was playing the piano jumped up from the stool, causing an empty beer can to fall off the piano. Tatum greeted the cats all around, then said, 'Drop that can again. It's a Pabst can, and the note it sounded was B-flat.'" Rozelle Gayle, one of Tatum's closest friends, tops this story by saying that Tatum could tell the key of any sound, including a toilet flushing.

Genius is an overworked word in this era of thunderous hyperbolic press agentry. Still, when one considers Arthur Tatum, there is no other proper descriptive adjective for referring to his talents. I have purposely pluralized them, for Tatum possessed several gifts—most of which remained unknown to all but a few of his best friends—his prodigious memory, his grasp of all sports statistics, and his skill at playing cards.

Art was a formidable opponent in all types of card games, although bid whist was his favorite. There are a few bridge champions still around who recall the fun they had when Tatum played with them. According to one's reminiscence, Art would pick up his cards as dealt, hold them about one inch from the good eye, adjust them into suits and from then on, never looked at his hand again. He could actually recall every card that was played, when, and by whom. Furthermore, he played his own cards like a master.

He had an incredible memory not only for cards but for voices and sounds as well. One account of his aptitude in catching voices has been told and retold. It seems that while playing London with Adelaide Hall back in the late thirties, he was introduced to a certain person and then immediately swept along the receiving line. Six years later, when he was playing in Hollywood, the person came to see Tatum. He greeted him with "Hello, Art. How are you? I'll bet you don't remember me," Tatum replied, "Sure, I remember you. Gee, you're looking good. I'm sorry I didn't get a chance to talk to you at that party in London. Your name is Lord So and So."

I realize that nature has a way of compensating for any inadequacy, but Tatum's abilities transcended ordinary compensation. With only a high school education, he was a storehouse of information. His favorite sports were baseball and football, followed by horseracing. Tatum could quote baseball pitchers' records, batting averages for almost all players in both big leagues, names and positions of football players, the game records for any year, and so forth. Tatum's close friend Rozelle Gayle recalls back in Art's Chicago days (the thirties) that all the musicians frequented the drugstore on the corner of Forty-seventh Street and South Park. Art became so respected as an authority on any subject (and that included population statistics) that the fellows would have him settle their arguments instead of telephoning a newspaper.

Despite impaired vision, he was a very independent man. He had little methods to avoid being helped. For example, he always asked the bank to give all his money in new five-dollar bills, which he put in a certain pocket. When he had to pay for something, he gave a five and then counted his change by fingering the one dollar bills and feeling the coins. The one's then went into a certain pocket and the coins into another. He had a mind like an adding machine and always knew exactly how much money he had.

One of the most significant aspects of Tatum's artistry stemmed from his constant self-challenge. At the piano, Art seemingly delighted in creating impossible problems from the standpoint of harmonies and chord progressions. Then he would gleefully improvise sequence upon sequence until the phrase emerged as a complete entity within the structure of whatever composition he happened to be playing. Many is the time I have heard him speed blithely into what I feared was a musical cul-de-sac, only to hear the tying resolution come shining through. This required great knowledge, dexterity, and daring. Tatum achieved much of this through constant practice, working hours every day on exercises to keep his fingers nimble enough to obey that quick, creative mind. He did not run through variations of songs or work on new inventions to dazzle his audiences. Rather, he ran scales and ordinary practice exercises, and if one didn't know who was doing the laborious, monotonous piano routines, he would never guess that it was a jazzman working out.

Another form of practice was unique with Tatum. He constantly manipulated a filbert nut through his fingers, so quickly that if you tried to watch him, the vision blurred. He worked with one nut until it became sleek and shiny from handling. When it came time to replace it, he would go to the market and feel nut after nut—a whole bin full, until he found one just the right size and shape for his exercises.

Art's hands were of unusual formation, though just the normal size for a man of his height and build. But when he wanted to, he somehow could make his fingers span a twelfth on the keyboard. The average male hand spans nine or ten of the white notes, eleven is considered wizard, but twelve is out of this world. Perhaps the spread developed from that seeming complete relaxation of the fingers—they never rose far above the keyboard and looked almost double-jointed as he ran phenomenally rapid, complex runs. His lightning execution was the result of all that practice, along with the instant communication between his fingers and brain.

His touch produced a sound no other pianist has been able to capture. The method he used was his secret, which he never revealed. The Steinway was his favorite piano, but sometimes he played in a club that had a miserable piano with broken ivories and sour notes. He would run his fingers over the keyboard to detect these. Then he would play that night in keys that would avoid as much as possible the bad notes. Anything he could play, he could play in any key.

With all that talent, perhaps it is not strange the effect that Art had on other pianists. When he went where they were playing, his presence made them uncomfortable. Some would hunt for excuses to keep from playing in front of the master. Others would make all kinds of errors on things that, under other circumstances, they could play without even thinking about it. There was the case of the young fellow who played a great solo, not being aware that Tatum was in the house. When Art congratulated him later, he fainted.

This sort of adulation did not turn Tatum's head, and he continually sought reassurance after a performance. Any friend who was present would be asked, "How was it?" One couldn't ask for more humility from a king of his instrument.

A little-known fact is that Art also played the accordion. Back in Ohio, before he had gained success, he was offered a year's contract in a night club if he would double on accordion. He quickly mastered the instrument and fulfilled the engagement, but he never liked the accordion, and after that gig, he never played it again.

Tatum always liked to hear other piano players, young or old, male or female. He could find something kind to say even about quite bad performers. Sometimes his companion would suggest leaving a club where the pianist could only play some clunky blues in one key. But Art would say, "No, I want to hear his story. Every piano player has a story to tell."

His intimates (two of whom—Eddie Beal and Rozelle Gayle—I thank for much of this information) agree that Tatum's favorites on the piano were Fats Waller, Willie (The Lion) Smith, and Earl Hines. He also liked lots of the youngsters, including Nat Cole, Billy Taylor, and Hank Jones.

In the days when most musicians enjoyed hanging out with each other, Art and Meade Lux Lewis palled around. Two more dissimilar chums could hardly be imagined. Tatum was a rather brooding, bearlike figure of a man, and Meade Lux was a plumper, jolly little fellow. They kept a running joke going between themselves, Meade Lux claiming that Art was cheap, even if Tatum was paying the tab.

Tatum's leisure hours began when almost everyone else was asleep, at 4:00 A.M. or so. He liked to sit and talk, drink and play, after he finished work. There was a serious and well-hidden side to the man. His secret ambition was to become known as a classical composer, and somewhere there exist fragments of compositions he put on tape for orchestration at some later date.

Tatum also wanted, very definitely, to be featured as a soloist accompanied by the Boston or New York symphony orchestras, which he considered among the world's best. As a matter of record, this admiration for the longer-haired musical forms was mirrored; he had numerous fans among classical players, who were astonished at his skill, technique, and imagination. To them, his gifts were supernatural. Vladimir Horowitz, who frequently came to hear Art play, said that if Tatum had taken up classical piano, he'd have been outstanding in the field.

It's been said that Tatum forced today's one-hand style of piano into being because after he'd finished playing all over the instrument with both hands, the only way for the piano to go was back, until the people forgot how much Tatum played.

Another of Art's ambitions, also unrealized, was to be a blues singer! He loved to relax by playing and singing the blues. He knew he didn't have much of a voice, but when he was offstage, he'd sing the blues. He had a feeling for the form but kept that side of himself well hidden from the public. He really adored Blind Lemon Jefferson, Bessie Smith, and, especially, Big Joe Turner.

Most musicians could never guess what Art was going to play from one moment to the next, which made the group he had with guitarist Tiny Grimes and bassist Slam Stewart unquestionably the best combo he ever had. The trio played on New York's Fifty-second Street around 1945. These three communicated, anticipated, and embellished each other as if one person were playing all three instruments. It was uncanny when it's considered that they never played it safe, never put in hours of rehearsal with each sequence pinpointed. On the contrary, every tune was an adventure, since nobody could predict where Art's mind would take them.

Tatum loved to go from one key to another without his left hand ever breaking the rhythm of his stride. Even in this, he was unpredictable, since he never went to the obvious transpositions, like a third above. No, Art would jump from B-flat to E-natural and make the listener love it.

While Art was alive, and as great as he was, there were still a few detractors. One such critic had been trained as a classical pianist but was trying desperately to apply his academic training to jazz. This fellow said, during one of Tatum's superb performances, "Sure, Art's great, but he fingers the keys the wrong way."

How sour can grapes get?

Another compatriot who used to haunt every place that Art played, night after night, made the public statement: "Good God! This Tatum is the greatest! Thank God he's black—otherwise nobody's job would be safe." I suspect there was a lot of truth in that remark.

Art never seemed to let the inequities of his situation bother him. Still, in the early morning when he had consumed a few cans of beer and was surrounded by his personal camp followers, he would unburden himself, asking, "Did you hear so-and-so's latest record? What a waste of wax, for Christ's sake! There must be over 2,000 fellows who can play more than this cat. But you see who he's recording for? It will probably sell half a million copies while Willie the Lion just sits back smoking his cigar, without a gig. When will it end?"

Tatum was a great crusader against discrimination, but in his own quiet way. He used to cancel engagements if he found that the club excluded colored persons. Loyalty to his friends, even when it was not advantageous to his career, was another strong point. (I recall the time I went to catch him at a club called the Streets of Paris, in Los Angeles. After a period of superlative enjoyment, I went to the piano to pay my respects and leave. But just as Art said, "Hello, how long have you been in the joint?" Cesar Romero and Loretta Young walked up. So I stepped back to let Art converse with the movie royalty. Art said, "Come on back here. I want to introduce you. Cesar, Loretta, I want you to meet Rex Stewart," and went on to build me up, undeservedly, till they asked for my autograph!)

Art was no glad-hander. He was polite, reserved, affable but not particularly communicative unless the conversation was about one of his hobbies. A more self-effacing person would be hard to find, and he was generous to a fault with his friends. Yet, he could summon up a tremendous amount of outraged dignity when it was called for.

Perhaps Art Tatum would have been assured a firmer place in musical history if he had not alienated too many of the self-right-eous aficionados who preferred their piano sounds less embroi-dered, less imaginative, and more orthodox. Therefore, it follows that Tatum would never be their favorite pianist. Posterity tends to prove that Art requires neither champion nor defense, since the proof of his genius remains intact and unblemished. The beauty within the framework of his music transcends the opinions of critics, aficionados, fans, and musicians themselves. History is the arbiter. For the truly great, fame is not fleeting but everlasting.

Down Beat, October 20, 1966

Appendix I

Count Basie

BY HSIO WEN SHIH

COUNT BASIE, the last of the great pianist-bandleaders of the swing era to gain popularity, was also the least obtrusive. He was not a composer of genius like Duke Ellington or a clever arranger like Fletcher Henderson or a virtuoso pianist like Earl Hines. He did not put his personality on display like Cab Calloway or "conduct" like Jimmie Lunceford. He sat at the piano, smiling modestly, giving out an occasional tinkle with so little fuss that a stranger might have asked what he *did*. Yet he was the leader of a band full of brilliant, individual soloists who swung together with a unique lift and power, a rhythmic unity that seemed like second nature. And almost all these individualists would have agreed that Basie was a great leader, though none could explain exactly why.

They would probably have agreed with what trombonist-arranger Johnny Mandel said many years later: Basie was a rhythmic catalyst. "The band doesn't feel good till he's up there," Mandel said. "He makes everybody play differently." Perhaps they would have agreed that he urged them to excitement by the tact and restraint of his own playing, by careful listening, by stringent control. At least guitarist Freddie Green recognized that "he contributes the missing things."

His tact and restraint were also important to the everyday life of the band on the road. "We'll be doing one-nighters," said one

Basie sideman, "and everything will be going wrong. The bus breaks down; there's no time for dinner; we get to work late; the promoter is angry. Basie couldn't be calmer or funnier." He kept the tensions from the players in the band, so that, as trumpeter Harry Edison said, "No matter what went wrong, it never got to the point where anybody in the band wouldn't feel like playing."

He treated his musicians with the same tact and restraint, so that they felt, as Buck Clayton explained, "Basie, a contemporary of ours, just happened to be the leader." All through the thirties and forties, Basie traveled on the bus with his sidemen, hung out with them after work, and shared their amusements. "We were all like brothers," singer Jimmy Rushing has recalled. And another man said, "Basie is still a sideman at heart. He doesn't think like a leader, at least not in terms of laying down the law; he's only the leader while he's on the stand."

Perhaps that was only natural. Basie had spent his journeyman years with the half-dozen men who became the nucleus of the band he brought out of Kansas City in 1936. They had all worked together as equals in the Southwest for nearly eight years. Basie's association with this group of musicians began in 1928, when he joined Walter Page's Blue Devils.

Bill Basie was originally an easterner, born in 1904 in Red Bank, New Jersey. He was taught to play piano by his mother when he was a child, and, after a fling at drumming, he continued to teach himself piano while he gigged around New Jersey and New York City. His family was poor but decent—his father was a gardener and his mother a domestic—so he went to work as a musician right out of high school. In his late teens, he played in New York with Elmer Snowden's band at the Nest Club, with June Clark in a Fourteenth Street dancehall, and with a band at Leroy's in Harlem. During these years, he came under the influence of Fats Waller, the enfant terrible of the organ who played for the silent movies at Harlem's Lincoln Theater. Through him, Basie picked up many of the stylistic tricks of the Harlem stride pianists. In 1923, he succeeded Waller as the pianist with Liza and Her Shuffling Sextet, Katie Crippens' vaudeville act, which included "a comic, singer, dancer, piano, drums, and maybe one horn." Basie actually had to beat out Duke Ellington—Ellington made his second trip to New York from Washington in the hope of getting the same job.

For the next four years, Basie worked in vaudeville as, so he says, "just a kinda honky-tonk piano player." He remembers hearing the Blue Devils for the first time in 1926, when he was passing through Tulsa, Oklahoma, with Gonzelle White's act on the Keith Circuit. He was astonished at their music. "At first I thought somebody in the hotel had some crazy records," he recalled, "but then I saw it—an advertising wagon down the street, plugging a dance. It turned out to be Walter Page and the Blue Devils. I chased after the band and got to know some of the cats; I finally wound up sitting in with them at a breakfast dance. Believe me, that was some music."

A year later, Basie was with an act called the Whitman Sisters that broke up in Kansas City, Missouri. He found work for the better part of a year playing for the silent movies at a ragged little side-street theater called the Eblon. Sometime during the summer of 1928, perhaps in Dallas and perhaps in Kansas City, Basie joined the Blue Devils.

The Blue Devils had been a road-show band led by Texas trombonist Ermir Coleman. When Coleman decided to retire from music, he turned the band over to its tuba player, Walter Page, who managed to keep the band going as a small group even after the road show folded.

In 1925, Page persuaded a group of Oklahoma City businessmen to back him in expanding the group into a big band. The new band was ragged and undisciplined; some of the men could not even read music. But Page, a big, heavy-set, sober-minded man, was an unusually well-trained musician for that time and place; he had studied music at Kansas University. He began to teach the men in the band to read and rehearsed them until they became unusually accurate ensemble players with exceptional discipline and group spirit.

He had an eye for talent, too, and he gradually added fine soloists to the band as they traveled—the men who were to be the nucleus of the Basie band.

In Oklahoma City he found blues singer Rushing; in Dallas he added alto and clarinet player Buster Smith; in Tyler, Texas, the trumpeter Oran (Hot Lips) Page; he stole trombonist-arranger Eddie Durham from Jesse Stone's band; and in 1930, during a tour north to Minnesota, he found the great tenor saxophonist Lester Young.

Although Page was only the nominal leader of the band—it was organized as a cooperative with all members sharing equally —his musical influence on the younger men was profound. Jo Jones, Basie's drummer, who met Page in the thirties, always insisted that "musically, Page was the father of Basie, Rushing, Buster Smith. . . ." And he added, "Page was a musical father to me, too, because without him I wouldn't have known how to play drums. For two years Page told me how to phrase. . . . Aside from that, Page also told me a few of the moral responsibilities that go into making up a musician's, an artist's, life."

Unfortunately, the music of the Blue Devils is preserved on only two 78-rpm recordings: *Blue Devil Blues* and a Basie riff tune called *Squabblin'*. But musicians who heard it in its prime say it was the most exciting band in the Southwest.

By 1928 the Blue Devils were considered the best band in a territory that included Texas, Oklahoma, and Kansas, and Page was eager to challenge the Bennie Moten Band, which monopolized the best jobs in Kansas City. Sometime during that year, the two bands met in a battle of music, and the Blue Devils played so well that Moten apparently offered to hire the band intact, including Page as music director, to play under Moten's name. Page turned down the offer, but Moten refused to be discouraged. He adopted the slower tactic of hiring away the better musicians among the Blue Devils one by one. He could offer better pay and a more settled life in Kansas City without the discomforts of life on the road.

Basie and Durham were the first to leave Page for Moten, in the summer of 1929. Jimmy Rushing came over in 1930 and Oran Page followed in 1931. That same year, Walter Page, discouraged by personnel problems and union trouble, turned the Blue Devils over to James Simpson and joined Moten.

Without Walter Page, the Blue Devils struggled on until 1933, sometimes dwindling down to five or six men but then gradually building back to twelve or thirteen. Finally, their instruments were seized by the police in West Virginia during a disastrous eastern tour, and the musicians had to hobo back to the Southwest on their own. Four of the survivors, including Buster Smith and Lester Young, eventually joined Moten's band. Moten had finally absorbed the Blue Devils.

"Bennie Moten," Oran Page once explained, "was a businessman first and last." But he was a politician as well, according to trumpeter Ed Lewis. "Pendergast was for him, and so was Judge Holland and Tommy Gershwin, the prosecuting attorney. His word meant a lot, and he was a big influence among a lot of people. Bennie never held any office, but whichever way he went, so did a lot of people."

Being close to Kansas City's Boss Tom Pendergast meant a great deal to a musician in those days. In spite of prohibition, in spite of the depression, Kansas City was a good town for musicians and entertainers. It was a wide-open town, the center of night-life for a large dry area of the Southwest, and as Mary Lou Williams explained, "Most of the night clubs were run by politicians and hoodlums. . . . Work was plentiful for musicians, though some of the employers were tough people."

According to Oran Page, "through contacts of this type, [Moten] was able to control all the good jobs and locations in and around Kansas City. In his day, you might say that he was stronger than MCA."

Moten's personal popularity with the Negro population also was good for business. Ed Lewis remembers that he had the pick of the social-club dances, "There were around 300 social clubs in Kansas City then, and they all gave dances in every part of the year."

Moten, as Oran Page hinted, wasn't especially good as a pianist or a musician, but he used all his political skill in dealing with the musicians in the band. "Bennie was cool," Jo Jones recalls. "He didn't browbeat his men. Whenever Bennie wanted something done, he'd call the band together, and he'd always speak softly

enough so that you had to hear him. After it was all over, he'd
produce a gallon of whiskey."

It must have been from Moten that Basie learned the importance of the gray virtues—consideration, tolerance and self-con-
trol—to the successful bandleader.

Moten's band had begun as a heavy version of a New Orleans
ensemble, somewhat muddied by the expanded instrumentation.
But with the leavening introduced by the former Blue Devils, and
particularly through the influence of Basie and Durham, the band
began to develop the dry, loose quality that distinguished the
Basie band six years later. By 1932, when the band traveled east
to cut its final records for Victor, it was playing with some of the
airy lift and the same even four-beat rhythm that Basie's band had
in maturity.

During that trip east. Moten decided to modernize the sound
of the band even more. He bought forty arrangements from two
arrangers, Fletcher Henderson's brother Horace and Benny Carter. These arrangements reinforced the lighter sound that the
Blue Devils had introduced, and some of the techniques of the
eastern arrangers were absorbed by the arrangers in the band—
especially Eddie Durham and, later, Buster Smith—to pass into
the common knowledge of Kansas City musicians and to re-
emerge in Basie's band five years later.

The years Basie spent with Moten were the years that most
Kansas City musicians remember so fondly, when jam sessions
started after work and lasted until afternoon, when, according to
Jo Jones, "You could be sleeping one morning at 6:00 A.M., and a
traveling band would come into town for a few hours, and they
would wake you up to make a couple-of-hours' session with them
until 8:00 in the morning"; when it wasn't unusual for one number to go on for an hour or an hour and a half. Although the last
of those good years, 1933, was in the depth of the depression,
Kansas City, because of the relaxed attitude of the politically cor-
rupt city fathers, remained an oasis in the dry central plains, the
city lights for a dozen states. Prosperity continued for musicians.

But repeal cut the economic base from Kansas City musicians.
In 1934, even Moten's band was beginning to feel the pinch.

Work became scarce, and during a job at the Cherry Blossom, the sidemen's dissatisfaction focused on a dispute about some expenses charged to them. They rebelled against Moten. When the dispute was over, Basie was leading the band at the Cherry Blossom, which included all but two members of Moten's band. Basie took them to Little Rock, Arkansas, to play a location date, but they drew few people. Moten found work again. One by one, the men went back to Moten. But Moten held no grudge; he hired Basie again, too.

When Moten died in 1935, his nephew Ira (Bus) Moten briefly took over as leader. By summer, however, Bill Basie turned bandleader again, this time more modestly, starting with five pieces at the Reno Club and gradually expanding to nine. At this point, Basie's journeyman years were coming to an end.

He had spent nearly eight years among the group of musicians Page had assembled. Through his contact with them, he had absorbed their feeling for the blues to add to his background in New York jazz. Although Basie had started as a rather "full" pianist in the James P. Johnson tradition, Moten's records show that by 1932 he had turned himself into a linear, single-note, right-hand pianist in the Earl Hines style, who let Page, now on string bass, take care of the bass line with absolute confidence.

As a bandleader, he had inherited from Page a group of musicians who knew each other thoroughly after the years with the Blue Devils and Moten. He had arrangers Durham and Smith. Perhaps most important, he had learned from Moten's example how to run a tight but happy band.

He was to have two years of scuffling with his band before his chance came. The band worked in a small club eight hours a night, six nights a week, and twelve hours on the other night. Leader's scale was twenty-one dollars a week, and sidemen got eighteen. But the Reno Club did have a remote wire, and the band broadcast every Sunday night over a local independent station.

In 1936 John Hammond, at the time a jazz writer and, as now, an enthusiast, heard one of these broadcasts while he was traveling with Benny Goodman's band. He became so enthusiastic over the vitality of the Basie band that he worked to bring the band to national notice.

Hammond went to Kansas City and introduced himself to Basie. He persuaded Basie that the band had to be expanded to fourteen pieces. One of the first new men was trumpeter Buck Clayton, who was passing through Kansas City with tenor saxophonist Herschel Evans on their way to join Willie Bryant's band in New York. Basie hired them both, Clayton to replace "Lips" Page, who had left during the Reno Club gig. The former Moten lead trumpeter, Ed Lewis, joined Clayton and Carl Smith in the trumpet section. Dan Minor and George Hunt were in the trombone section. Evans joined Lester Young in the reeds. Jo Jones and Walter Page held the rhythm section together.

Meanwhile, Hammond persuaded Goodman to come and listen to the band. Goodman was enthusiastic and enlisted the help of his own booking agent, Willard Alexander. Alexander began to find the band bookings outside Kansas City; Hammond began thinking about record contracts. But Basie was still naive about the band business. He signed a contract with Decca to record twenty-four sides for a flat $750 with no royalties.

The first job for the band outside of Kansas City was at the Grand Terrace in Chicago. It was a disaster. The band was used to playing head arrangements of blues and riff tunes, and at the Grand Terrace it had to play a show.

"They had us playing *The Poet and Peasant Overture* as our big show number," Basie recalled. "The band just didn't make it, and there was nothing in the show that gave us a real chance to display ourselves properly."

Chicago audiences didn't take to Basie's blues, and the band was saved only by Fletcher Henderson's generosity—he lent Basie his whole book of pop tunes. (When Basie opened in New York City later, he had to buy stock arrangements of show tunes and Latin dance music.)

"Some of the Kansas City guys had to be fired," Buck Clayton remembered. "They faked pretty well until we had to cut the show music at the club. Then it was all over for them."

The rhythm section was solid, and Clayton and Evans were immediately recognized as fine soloists, but the musicianship of the band was severely criticized. One critic wrote, "If you think the trumpets are out of tune, you should listen to the trombones. If you think the trombones are out of tune, you should listen to the reeds."

Basie didn't panic. He coolly began to tinker with the personnel. He needed better musicianship, but he knew that he had to retain the best qualities of his Kansas City band—its looseness in ensemble playing, its best and most characteristic soloists, its blues-based riff style and surging rhythm. He began to hire some highly professional eastern musicians to stiffen up the musicianship. He brought in Billie Holiday as girl singer.

Hammond and Alexander sent the band on the road to tighten up, but conditions were hardly ideal for polishing a band. Billie Holiday recalled, "We'd play a whole string of riff-raff joints, rough Negro dance halls in the South where people were sneaking in corn whiskey from across the tracks, and then, boom, in the middle of this grind we would be booked into some big white hotel. "We didn't have the right uniforms, clothes, equipment— the cats in the band didn't have the right horns they needed— we'd all be beat from traveling thousands of miles with no sleep, no rehearsal, and no preparation—and yet we'd be expected to be real great."

Basie showed his quality as a leader then, keeping everyone happy, keeping the band moving, somehow holding everyone's loyalty through impossible disasters.

The New York opening at Roseland was another disaster. Fortunately, Goodman, Hammond, and Alexander were able to persuade the manager to keep the band on despite the obvious difficulties it had pleasing the white dancers. Basie stayed cool as ever and concentrated on the musical side.

Clayton said, "New York wasn't easy. The band scuffled, and it starved. But it didn't seem to matter. Playing was the important thing. Sticking together and making a go of the band was our ambition. We wouldn't think of leaving Basie no matter how good the offers were."

Finally, almost three years after Basie started scuffling with his band, they managed to satisfy the listeners at the Famous Door on Fifty-second Street. During that year the band scored a dramatic victory over Chick Webb's band during a battle of music at the Savoy Ballroom. They were the first band to outplay Webb's on his home ground, and their future in New York was assured.

By the time the personnel of the band stabilized, the trumpets were Ed Lewis, Buck Clayton, Harry Edison, and Shad Collins; the trombones were Dan Minor, Benny Morton, and the witty ringer, Dickie Wells; the reeds were Jack Washington, Earle Warren, Lester Young, and Herschel Evans. The rhythm section still included Page and Jo Jones, but the guitarist was the rock-steady Freddie Green who joined in New York. Jimmy Rushing and Helen Humes were the vocalists.

During the next years, this magnificent band made a series of records, at first for Decca and later for Columbia, that remain among the greatest delights of swing. The arrangements were usually simple—often no more than a sketch made up of riffs based on such jam-session favorites as the blues, *I Got Rhythm,* and *Diga Diga Doo.* The rhythm section was flexible and steady, with a delightful and novel subdivision of labor among the four men that supported and propelled the sparkling and ardent solo work of Clayton, Edison, Wells, Evans, and Young. The records have retained their vigor and luster. The earliest records, such as *Roseland Shuffle* and *Pennies from Heaven,* are marred by sloppy ensemble playing, but by late 1938—on records such as *Rock-a-bye Basie, Sent for You Yesterday,* and *Panassie Stomp*—the band was beginning to play with security and definition. The peak came in the magnificent Columbia series of 1939 and 1940.

By the time the United States entered the war, the band had begun to change. Evans had died; Young and Wells had left; Clayton and Jones were snatched eventually by the Army. But Basie seemed to have the knack for finding exactly the right replacements; Buddy Tate for Evans, Don Byas for Young; Vic Dickenson for Wells; Shadow Wilson for Jones.

Basie managed to keep going all through the war, though records like *Taps Miller* and *Little Beaver* show a slight tightening in ensemble work. But men such as Young, who often contributed heads, or Clayton, who wrote arrangements, were gone. Basie began to rely on outside arrangers, and the rapid turnover of personnel during the war made written arrangements more important than ever. Arrangers, such as Buster Harding and Jimmy Mundy, rather than the soloists, began to dominate the band, and the informal, improvised character of Basie's music started to evaporate.

Basie managed to survive the slump that flattened the band business after the war, but in 1949, he discovered that he was losing money, going into debt to keep the band going. He had always been careless about business matters, and he had no savings to fall back on. He disbanded.

By then he had in the band several young men who had been influenced by the beboppers, and in 1950 he formed an octet built around young soloists of similar musical conceptions—trumpeter Clark Terry, clarinetist Buddy DeFranco, tenor saxophonist Wardell Gray, baritone saxophonist Serge Chaloff. Working with the small group, he managed to recoup his financial position.

Like the Reno Club band, this octet was primarily a soloist's band, but the few records it made during the next year show signs of a fresh approach to ensemble work that might have been developed. Unfortunately, when Basie decided to re-form a big band in 1951, he did not build on the possibilities of this small group as he had in 1936. The second Basie band was the work of arrangers, with Basie serving as editor-in-chief. The music varied with the arrangers. Johnny Mandel produced stiffer versions of prewar Basie arrangements; Neal Hefti, who had been with Woody Herman, produced some lyrical and finely crafted medium-tempo scores; Ernie Wilkins contributed some kindergarten blues.

The expanded brass section, which gave the arrangers more chance for harmonic complexity, began to outweigh the reeds. The band became what Basie had promised it never would be—raucous. A chunky and stomping drummer gave the rhythm section a heavy, doughy sound. The soloists, except for trumpeters

Joe Newman and, later, Thad Jones, were only competent players who understood their style rather than musicians of genuine individuality and expressive quality.

In 1955, Basie added a new blues singer, Joe Williams, and suddenly found that he had a hit record on his hands, a blues called *Every Day.* Although Williams is a leaden and heavy-footed singer, given to steady hammering rather than expressive phrasing, he gave Basie an enormous audience among the rock-and-roll fans who were the largest public for records. The success was followed by several more—another Williams blues, *The Come-back,* and a boring instrumental that belabored *April in Paris.* The band had become what André Hodeir called a machine for swinging, more like the precision drill team of Jimmie Lunceford than the collection of individualists Basie led during the thirties and forties.

During the last few years, however, there have been new signs of life in the Basie band. Some of the men in the band began to accept the basically heavy quality of the band and wrote arrangements that exploit the density of sound. Before he left the band, saxophonist Frank Foster did several arrangements, beginning with *Shiny Stockings,* that contrast the heavy ensemble with the openness of the solos. Thad Jones also wrote a few brilliant arrangements for the band. It was a hint that there was a future for the Basie band beyond neo-swing.

But Basie has become increasingly conservative about trying out new tunes and seems to prefer to stick to well-tested arrangers. However, he commissioned several sets of arrangements by Benny Carter, and their collaboration seems to combine the mobility of the 1939 Basie band with the power of the postwar edition. But it may be too late. There are rumors that Basie is tired of the strenuous life of the road and is talking of retirement. But some of the men in the band say it is only talk.

"They'll carry him back from a road trip one day," one of them said. "He's like Louis. He's too used to the road to quit now."

Appendix II

Rex William Stewart, Jr.

BY FRANCIS THORNE

THE WORLD has many takers and few givers. Men who are considerate of the people with whom they come in contact often are described by those who know them as "human." When one of these men happens to be a great musician as well as an articulate and intelligent person, the result is, of necessity, an unusual being. To write about Rex Stewart is to have an opportunity to explore a personality who is at once complex and understandable, always sympathetic and fascinating. It must be stated at the outset that Rex is a close personal friend and that it is impossible to write this article completely objectively. But my hope is to delineate an important man in his chosen profession with the added dimension of respect and affection that comes from a close association over the past five years.

When I first met Rex, he was well-known to me as a wonderful cornetist and Ellington soloist whose *Boy Meets Horn* I had known by heart for many years. I always am inhibited when I meet a famous musician, particularly when I have admired him. It comes as a complete surprise, even after going through it a number of times, to find that the personality who has such a distinct professional character is, in reality, a human being who is sitting there and talking and feeling and being a little bit inhibited, too. This latter quality was the one that surprised me most about Rex the first few times we met. I had expected such dynamic assurance from having heard such music-making as those driving solos on Ellington's *Main Stem*. The fact that Rex was essentially modest, highly sensitive, and perhaps even had a bit of an inferiority complex, was almost a shock to me.

I was preoccupied, during the early organization meetings that led to the formation of the Great South Bay Festival, trying to make an analytical observation of this personality whom I had just met. But I had to realize that what I had mistaken for indecision, shyness, and lack of interest was nothing of the kind, but rather an intense desire to be tolerant, reasonable, and fair in decisions that had to be made. Rex weighed the importance of problems with the greatest care, but once a decision had been made, it was really interesting to see the enthusiasm and sureness with which he accomplished what he had set out to do.

I heard him frankly admit mistakes as soon as he made them. I saw him hire a practically unknown and very modern pianist [Cecil Taylor] without batting an eye after hearing one of his records for two or three minutes, maintaining that youth and originality have to be encouraged. I even heard him calm down an audience that was disappointed in a mediocre performance by telling a few jokes, then playing dazzlingly. I saw him refuse to accept money due him when the Great South Bay Festival was in the red. I saw him trying to have Don Redman take charge of conducting the first meeting of the Fletcher Henderson Alumni Band, because he honestly thought Redman was better suited for this conducting job than he was. Once, when Rex was forced to take on this irksome task himself, I saw him accomplish it decisively in spite of the enormous difficulties and obstacles he encountered.

All this is typical of Rex Stewart. Through his music and personality, he has contributed considerably to the world in which he has lived for fifty-three[*] years without receiving in exchange the reward that he justly deserves. After a musical career of more than forty years, Rex hasn't made a solid place for himself despite the fact that he has as much talent today as ever. This is the price of altruism, and it is what makes Rex and other jazz musicians

[*]I.e., in 1960 [Ed.]

bitter and cynical. This is the only sad comment we can make on the current jazz scene. Bitterness and cynicism are part of Rex's personality and others in his generation. But in his case, his own fundamental honesty emphasizes this less pleasant aspect of his personality. A jazz musician, above all, must be honest—if he's not, he's through. Perhaps a marked sense of humor helps a musician withstand the injustices of his environment, and certainly it is an integral part of his musical style.

Before going into an analysis of Rex's music and the influences that he underwent and caused, before looking into his other interests in life, it seems fair to briefly sketch his biographical profile. Rex was born in a family in which his music and other cultural activities had their importance, especially for his mother. Jane Johnson had met Rex's father in Bryn Mawr, Pennsylvania, at a concert of religious music where Rex, Sr., sang in a quartet from Lincoln University. He helped support his studies by singing and occasionally working in restaurants—waiting on tables, playing the piano, violin, mandolin. Jane played the piano well and began giving Rex, Jr., lessons when he was only four. Rex remembers that the pillar of the family was his maternal grandmother, Angelina Denby Johnson, the daughter of a Negro, Edwin Denby, and of an American Indian, Angelina Ricketts (whose Indian name, Ome-a-was-o, meant "morning song"). Angelina Ricketts was one of the first non-white girls admitted to a Quaker school and had a certain inclination toward reciting poetry. People said she was mystical because she was born with a caul. Her daughter, Rex's grandmother, was an invalid and spent her life in an armchair, making herself, for the most part, unbearable.

Yet Rex loved his grandmother because she read him poetry and often convinced his parents to give him sweets. She had a volume of poetry published in Philadelphia and was the author of hymns, for which she wrote the lyrics as well as the music. She taught mixed classes of whites and Indians and, as Rex says, "She had enough strength left over to have eleven children, of whom my mother was the youngest, and to educate them all."

Rex was introduced to prejudice through his grandmother. One day when Rex was five, his grandmother saw a white man passing on the stairs of the Weather Observatory near their house, and while Rex was playing, she let out a cry of the Indian war chant that nearly scared the imprudent passerby to death. She called him "dirty white traitor" and "white trash," still crying the war chant. Every time Rex hears "the rebel yell" again, he remembers the unusual old woman.

His grandmother played the organ very well, and it was often Rex's job to work the bellows. It seems that she always called him "boy," perhaps because she couldn't forgive his being half Negro. She took care of advancing Rex's "education" on the subject of racial discrimination, shouting at him, "Get out, you little nigger, your father's black and so are you. You'll never amount to anything." Then she cried the Indian war chant as "Whoo-oo-oo-nigger, nigger, nigger." Her husband was a Negro, and Rex thinks those outbursts were due to her pride in having Indian blood in her veins—but there was also her disappointment at being discovered doing something as prohibited as smoking.

Rex inherited his gentle soul from his maternal grandfather. When Rex was a little boy, his family had some Irish neighbors. One day one of the neighbors asked Rex's father if they could borrow a violin for a party to be given that night. Rex's grandfather gave them one which belonged to a certain Uncle Jacob, and, turning to Rex, admitted that they would never see that violin again, because the Irish would surely get drunk and get into a fight; the violin would end up in a thousand pieces. Of course, this is just what happened, and Rex asked, knowing from the beginning how it would end, why he lent the violin anyway. His grandfather answered, "Because they needed it." The next day, the Irishman came back with the bad news, offering to pay for the damage, but Rex's grandfather refused, saying he was happy to have been helpful and said that everything happened according to the will of the Lord. This episode left a strong impression on the small boy.

From another uncle, Fred, young Rex inherited his passion for fun and adventure. One day, this uncle managed to escape from the police during a riot, finding refuge in an attic under some rugs. Then, jumping from roof to roof, he wound up in a cemetery where he hid until nightfall. Once it got dark he stole a sheet hung out to dry, and, masquerading as a ghost, he managed to get out of town. He jumped on a train, which took him to Bridgeport. There he hid in the hold of a ship, which brought him to Baltimore, and from Baltimore he returned to Washington on foot!

We have fewer details about his parents, because Rex is reluctant to talk about them. It seems that the piano lessons were, above all, occasions for continual fights, because at that time Rex was more interested in playing with his friends than in studying music.

After a two-year struggle, his instruction was taken over by a professional teacher, a lady who appeared sweet and gentle enough, although she beat him with a ruler "with the enthusiasm of a football player." It then became his father's turn, and Rex's interest shifted from the piano to the violin. After a year of lessons, ten times more boring because they had the disadvantage of being taught by a father, everything ended when his parents divorced.

Rex's father always wanted his son to become a minister but after the divorce, a Georgetown police officer (J. Arthur Johnson) started a boys' band and succeeded in becoming responsible for Rex's musical education. Rex began his career on a bass cornet and was promoted to regular cornet within a few months. Before the police officer's death, he had become first cornetist. Those three years in the band constitute Rex's true musical training. The band played in concerts, parades, and churches. Its last performance occurred at the funeral of Officer Johnson, where the bandmembers cried so much they could hardly play.

Six months later, Rex joined a band led by the trombonist Danny Day, who had played with him in the Johnson band. Let's have Rex himself tell it: "Danny played ragtime with a melodic dixieland section. After I had been with him for a while, I learned pieces like *All by Myself in the Morning, Walking the Dog,* and many others. I remember the first one I learned to play. It was called *Cuban Moon*. When Day left for Europe, I started playing with the Ollie Blackwell Clowns. For that reason, I had to leave Washington at the age of fourteen. We started traveling with a musical review called *Go-Get-It,* but something terrible happened in Philadelphia, and we were left with nothing. I was lucky—after three weeks of living on two-for-a-nickel sandwiches, I happened to play in a jam session where I was noticed by the famous clarinetist Willie Lewis. He introduced me to Mr. Spiller of the Musical Spillers. I had to learn to play the saxophone, but the pay was fifty dollars a week, a very considerable sum for a kid my age. There my childhood ends."

We have a great description of this period by Elmer Snowden, leader of the Washingtonians with whom Duke Ellington took his first steps in the musical field: "I saw Rex for the first time," says Snowden, "in Washington in 1920, when I had the most famous band in the whole town. One night, while we were playing at Murray's, a young people's band happened to audition. It was a crazy group of kids led by a pianist whose name was Ollie [Blackwell]. They named themselves The Clowns Band, and they played sitting on the floor or jumping on the piano. We didn't think much of them, but two stood out; Bernard Addison and that kid in short pants who played the trumpet, maybe not very well, but with tremendous volume.

"Well, years went by and I saw Rex again in New York. Meanwhile, the Washingtonians had split up, and I played in a club called Balconades. Jimmie Harrison, my trombonist, told me that now Rex played very well. I didn't want to believe him, but Jimmie insisted so much that I told him to have him come so I could listen to him. This happened in 1923; as soon as I heard him play I took him in my band, where he stayed until 1926, the year in which I got him into Fletcher Henderson's band. When I say 'I got him into Henderson's band,' I'm telling the truth, because he would never have left me on his own, not even with a higher salary in view nor for the honor of taking Armstrong's place in the greatest and most famous band of the moment."

Rex continues the story of that period: "One night, Louis,

Henderson, and Big Green came to the Nest Club to listen to me. What a night! The outcome was that when Louis returned to Chicago, I was called to substitute for him. I stayed with Henderson for about eight months, until the hard work of always having to play like Louis, imitating his enormous range, made me tell Henderson that I had to go back to Washington because my grandmother was sick, which wasn't true. It was then that Tommy Ladnier was hired, and finally, Fletcher's wife, Leora, sent me to join Horace Henderson in Wilberforce, Ohio.

"One night, we drove in four cars from Louisville to New York between Sunday and Monday night. As soon as we arrived, Fletcher's wife told us that we had an engagement in Lexington, Kentucky, the next day, Tuesday! Without eating or sleeping, we bought a little gin and off with the cars again. As soon as we arrived, we began to play, but at the end of it we were all dead.

"Another time, in New York, at Roseland, we were beaten by Jean Goldkette's Victor band, which made us leave the bandstand with its beautiful arrangements of *Valencia* and *Baby Face*. They played with so much enthusiasm that we had to wait for hours to get on stage for our turn. Until that night, we had done the same thing opposite other bands; everybody was breathless to listen to us until that night when the Victor band arrived."

Stewart returned to Fletcher in 1929 to stay with him until 1933, except for a brief period between the end of 1930 and the beginning of 1931, during which time he played with McKinney's Cotton Pickers. Leaving Henderson, he tried to get together a small group under his name, but the enterprise was short-lived and unsuccessful. After a brief period with Louis Russell, who once had a famous band which was now on its way toward decline, Rex arrived at the decisive turning point of his career.

When Rex was invited by Duke Ellington to play in his famous band (which at that time was named Famous), Cootie Williams already was the first solo trumpeter, but Rex decided to accept, even though his swing style wasn't exactly right for the subtle arrangements and for the way-out Ellington band. The success of this decision is now jazz history, and we can certainly say that

Rex is one of the most authoritative and important voices in a band in which every musician is a star. If Rex had reached maturity playing with Henderson, the eleven years he spent with Ellington added a new dimension to his playing and allowed him to devote himself to composition, so that from this experience there emerges a musician in all respects more complete.

In 1945, after he left Ellington, Rex was signed by Norman Granz for his Jazz at the Philharmonic concert tours. Then, after some time, he devoted himself to a series of trips around the world with various small groups under his name, and he was the first American bandleader to bring his group on European tours after World War II.

Meanwhile, he had played feature parts in two films, *Syncopation* in Hollywood and *Affair in July* in France. Still in France, in 1948, he had the occasion to give a series of lectures on "Jazz, Original American Art Form" at the Paris Music Conservatory and to study gastronomy at the Cordon Bleu (cooking still is one of his favorite pastimes). In 1949, he opened new horizons in Australia (still with his group), giving a series of lectures at the University of Melbourne and going on tour of almost the whole continent.

In 1951, Rex decided to retire to a farm near Troy, New York, and during this period he realized that it is impossible to completely abandon the world of music. The appointments as musical director at the two radio stations in Troy are due to this conviction. In 1954, he returned to playing still more frequently, even if he didn't completely leave his farm. In 1955, he received the award, "The Longplaying Record of the Year," from John Wilson, the jazz critic of the *New York Times*. The following year, he reappeared on the New York scene, playing with a group of which he was the leader. This led him to be signed by a group of admirers on the south shore of Long Island. The nucleus expanded and gave life to the Great South Bay Jazz Festival, of which Rex was the musical director for the two years of the Festival's life, 1957 and 1958.

For two years, from 1957 to 1959, Rex was the first solo trumpeter in the swing band at Eddie Condon's club in New York. Even though this type of experience didn't much suit Stewart's rich and original style, he constituted for that orchestra a sweeping force and was the best soloist of importance that Condon ever had. From time to time, Rex made television appearances, and he finally had occasion to record frequently and with small groups which fit him, something that hadn't happened for a long time. Last year he tried to keep a quintet alive for regular work in night clubs, but the latest news I have is that they aren't very good as far as cash receipts go, even though this quintet has made several longplaying records.

We already know that Rex could play "forte." That he was full of swing from the beginning is certain. "For a while, I was influenced by Johnny Dunn," says Rex. "Then I heard Jimmie Harrison swing, although I really dug trumpet men like Tommy Morris and Jack Hatton, who was king of Harlem when I arrived in 1921. Coming up fast and copying Hatton was Bubber Miley, so I copied Bubber until I heard Louis Armstrong's records. The ones that Louis recorded with Joe Oliver impressed me the most. Also, I have to thank my buddy Happy Caldwell who taught me a lot. He was from Chicago and had come up in that hard-swinging school. Then there was Joe Smith, Bix Beiderbecke and Reuben Reeves—all these fellows played the most wonderful horns."

The Armstrong influence is very strong in Rex's four-bar solo breaks in the medium-tempo blues *Saint Louis Shuffle*, recorded by the Fletcher Henderson Orchestra in early 1927, during his first period with the band. Already the strong rhythmic drive and heavy on-the-beat accents can be heard, and there is considerable intensity such as Bubber Miley must have inspired in his followers. It would be hard to identify the player for certain, however.

By 1931, when Rex was already well on the way to maturity, the Henderson band recorded *Roll On, Mississippi, Roll On,* a popular one-step of the day. It is a commercial record made for dancing with an atrocious vocal chorus, but it is memorable because of a wonderful Coleman Hawkins solo and a muted trumpet obbligato played by Rex in the second sixteen bars of the first chorus. He swings over the saxophone section with authority and bite. The hot style of Louis can still be heard, but the more clipped phrases of the later Stewart are becoming noticeable. This is a very good solo. Technique is wonderfully developed. As a matter of fact, Elmer Snowden says that Rex "developed an amazing technique when he was with me (1923–1926) that seems to me to have been the foundation of such later men as Dizzy and Roy."

As Louis' successor in the Henderson band, he also developed more high-note technique after 1926. On the 1932 Henderson record of *Sugar Foot Stomp*, Rex is heard in his interesting rendition of the original Joe Oliver choruses from *Dippermouth*, and Stewart's tremendous swing puts him right alongside his predecessor. The warmth and intensity of his tone are most compelling today, and a strong personality can be felt even in this reproduction. Fascinatingly different is the second chorus of *Singing the Blues*, also from 1932. Here the Bix Beiderbecke creation is faithfully reproduced with the addition of a tone so warm that it does in fact sound like Stewart. This beauty of tone is a forecast of the ravishing sound that Rex was to get from his cornet eight years later in Ellington's *Dusk*.

By 1932, Rex had grown in the qualities of imagination and logical direction that are now associated immediately with a Stewart solo. These rapidly-developing characteristics can be heard in *My Sweet Tooth Says I Wanna* and *Moan You Moaners* (1931). After Stewart joined Ellington, it was not long before the great maestro was featuring his new virtuoso. At the first recording date after Rex's arrival, March 15, 1935, two unusual sides were recorded with small groups, *Tough Truckin'* and *Indigo Echoes*. This is a slightly more subtle Stewart, and the sides are important because their success, musically speaking, led to many small-band sides in the later thirties, some of the best of which carried the name of Rex Stewart as leader.

By 1936, Duke was writing his first real concerto-type composition for Rex, *Trumpet in Spades,* which showed off the fine technique of the instrumentalist. But even in 1936, the Beiderbecke influence is still strong in **Kissing My Baby Goodnight**. This influence, which never really has left Rex, is normally stronger in the more melodic tunes, but I find that here it is possible to say, "This is Rex Stewart playing." By this time, other factors may be apparent in his playing, but he still is swinging madly, as particularly in the last chorus of *Trumpet in Spades*.

Rex's position in jazz history would have been strong by this time, but the next two years were to see a new development which perhaps gives Rex the crowning touch to his style. Certainly it helped to make him sound so individual and exciting that he began to be felt more and more as a dynamic influence on other trumpet players who were then coming up. The thing came about this way, in the words of the inventor himself: "In about 1937, Duke had a rather serious operation which caused a lay-off for all the band. I did not have anything much to do one day, so I picked up the axe and started blowing. The valves were sorta sticky from not being in use, and caused me to produce a tone related to concert G instead of C. This was for all intents and purposes the G-sound on the horn, but it sounded like it was being heard through a fog! I liked the sound so I tried to find other sounds or notes that would relate to the G, enough to form a sequence, and, sure as you please, after a half hour or so, I found a few more. Then I got excited and called Duke at the hospital and tried to explain what I had discovered. Duke was always on the alert for off-beat facets of original music, and told me to bring the horn down, and that very next day *Boy Meets Horn* was in the works. At this point, I would like to say that I do not claim to have invented anything but the style, because I am sure that many more valves have become stuck before mine." This natural modesty of the man is typical.

Boy Meets Horn was recorded in September, 1938, and shows the valuable talent for composition that Rex Stewart possesses. Of course, Ellington was marvelous at bringing out the talents of his associates, and this was a collaboration. However, Rex must be recognized fully for his contribution to the invention of the half-valve usage, and then in the execution, which to this day is a wonder. I had the privilege of accompanying Rex in this number, along with Sonny Greer and Hayes Alvis, on a television show, and I was so intrigued that I could hardly remember to play on several occasions. This tune, with Rex in command, must be heard in order to savor fully the essence of his style.

One of the most hauntingly beautiful of the Ellington-Stewart compositions was the tune *Morning Glory*, recorded in 1940. Rex still has traces of the Beiderbecke influence, but, of course, it is nobody but Rex. His open-horn sound and his gentle, lyrical phrasing are models of fine taste and musicianship. This has been a special favorite of mine since it was first issued.

An example of Rex at his hottest and swingingest during the heyday of the Ellington band can be found in *Main Stem*, one of the most powerful big-band records that I have ever heard. His solo, early on Billy Strayhorn's *Take the A Train*, is a classic of its kind. The half-valve technique is also heard to fine advantage in another record made about the time of *Boy Meets Horn*— *Braggin' in Brass*, also a good example of the whole Ellington trumpet section in amazing unison passages, a mass virtuosity that has to be heard to be believed.

The small-band recordings made by the Ellington sidemen during the late thirties created a relaxed atmosphere for these men to work in, and often the compositions were written by the leader on the date. Some delightful, informal sides resulted from Rex's sessions, and these were always musically interesting. For example, on *Rexatious,* a composition of Stewart's in a medium-fast tempo, Rex is very relaxed and his muted tone has great warmth. In another Stewart composition, *Lazy Man's Shuffle* Stewart shows how great a rhythmic drive he can generate at a rather slow tempo. *Swing, Baby, Swing* indicates that Stewart was still indebted to Armstrong, in the way he hits the first three beats of a measure right on the button, and the perky little coda at the very end of the record is a delight. I think that Rex sounds most like himself when he plays with an open bell, and this Stewart sound is well heard in *Fat Stuff Serenade,* an unusually happy improvization on a tune attributed to Ellington and Stewart.

It is interesting to know that Rex himself goes out of his way to mention four people who played major roles in his life and who had some sort of strong influence on him. Elmer Snowden, his early friend, is responsible for helping Rex generally as a musician, but Rex recalls that it was the art of self-discipline which was the most valuable quality that he learned from Snowden. He gives credit to Mrs. Isabelle Spiller who talked him into taking up the alto saxophone. She taught him how to take care of himself as a very young man in a difficult world. Fletcher Henderson is mentioned by Rex with considerable feeling. It was apparent during the first reunion of the Henderson men in 1957 that it was a particularly emotional experience for Rex, as well as many of the others. Rex always remembers Smack for exposing him to the big-band idiom under the most favorable circumstances.

Duke Ellington, in whose orchestra Rex played so brilliantly, is the man whom Rex credits with having taught him to think creatively in a musical sense. It is important to know just what Rex has to say on this subject: "I really cannot venture a guess as to how much Ellington influenced me—perhaps more than even I am aware of or can bear to admit. But I do feel that the man, as a leader, was so magnificently gifted with so much open-mindedness and eagerness, so keenly analytical of the sounds and the impressions and moods created by combinations of various instruments that if he was the artist, we, of course, were the palette.

"At rehearsal he would always indicate the solos, saying to whomever he felt the solo was best suited, 'Take it in such-and-such a way.' Then he might say, 'Go again.' After we had played the tune down, he might take us over to the piano and then perhaps remark, 'What you are doing is OK, but to me it could be more savage, or more tender,' such as the case might have been.

"After about five years of that kind of exposure, I began to see why, when the critics would roast him for hiring anyone, Duke would merely say, 'That's what I want.' I marveled at the wisdom of the man who knew what he wanted. OK, I concede. I was not only influenced, but also will remain influenced."

Ellington used to delight audiences by engaging Rex in "conversations" during which Rex would almost make his horn talk. This can be called another Stewart invention. It is one of the most amusing and amazing tricks, and can be heard on a recent RCA album that Rex made with Dickie Wells called *Chatter Jazz.* The conversation between the two of them at the beginning of *Lets Do It* had me in convulsions the first time I heard it. This album shows the 1959 Rex Stewart as a completely personal musician with great imagination, tender lyricism, and blazing swing. He is a man still at the peak of his musicianship with plenty to say and the ability to say it. Another fine example of present day Stewart can be found on the *Porgy and Bess Revisited* album on the Warner Brothers label. The characters are portrayed by jazz musicians, and Rex is cast as Sportin' Life. *It Ain't Neccessarily So* shows just about every facet of Rex's musicianship.

The United Artists recording of the Henderson reunion in concert during the second year's performance is very disappointing in some respects, but, it shows Rex in two very complimentary lights. His extended composition is full of lovely melodic ideas and is proof that as a composer Stewart is still highly creative and sensitive. Another highlight is his performance of *These Foolish Things,* a solo taken at slow ballad tempo and with an open bell. I remember well the moment this performance transpired. A younger musician had played this tune quite well earlier in the evening. Rex had been plagued by many events during the course of the day that would have discouraged most people to the point of "throwing in the towel," but he rose above them. Then, finally, when the Henderson band came on and sounded ragged, Rex suddenly seemed to get a look of determination on his face and decided that the Henderson performance had to be saved. The man was mad and figured that he would gamble the moment by betting on himself alone, followed by two other reliable and brilliant soloists—Hilton Jefferson and Dickie Wells. The results are on record. Rex played a solo accompanied by rhythm alone with an intensity and a command that was almost awe-inspiring. The rest of the concert went well, but I will always remember this particular solo and often pull out the record and listen.

It is a good insight into a man to know which people in his field he singles out as being true artists. I asked Rex to do this, and the results are as follows:

Trumpet: Bunny Berigan, Russell Smith, Joe Smith, Bobby Hackett, Bobby Stark, Dizzy Gillespie, Roy Eldridge, Charlie Shavers, Alvin Alcorn, Bix Beiderbecke.

Trombone: J. C. Higginbotham, Jack Jenny, Tommy Dorsey, Jimmie Harrison, Sandy Williams, George Troop, Abe Lincoln, Lawrence Brown, Cutty Cutshall.

Tenor Sax: Dick Wilson, Chu Berry, Coleman Hawkins, Babe Russin, Bud Freeman, Happy Caldwell, Ben Webster, Al Sears.

Alto Sax: Johnny Hodges, Benny Carter, George Johnson, Charlie Parker.

Baritone Sax: Gerry Mulligan, Harry Carney, Pinkie Williams.

Bass Sax: Joe Rushton, Johnny Dengler.

Piano: Art Tatum, Marty Napoleon, Red Richards.

Drums: Sid Catlett, Dave Tough, Roy Bournes.

Guitar: Eddie Lange, Oscar Aleman, Bucky Pizzarello, Django Reinhardt.

Bass: Lennie Gaskin, Charlie Mingus, Arvill Shaw.

In 1958, Rex was elected to membership in the American Society of Composers, Authors and Publishers (ASCAP). He has been creating tunes, mostly improvised, for over forty years and finally this recognition came. I often listen to the incredible junk that passes for popular music nowadays, and I reflect upon the gold mine of melodies that were created by Rex and his many jazz cohorts on the spur of the moment and forgotten because no recording apparatus was listening. There is justice in Rex Stewart's membership in ASCAP. There is little justice in the difficult time many musicians of this stature have in making a decent living. Perhaps there is solace for them in knowing that many hundreds and thousands of listeners have had their lives made brighter by their work over the years. No matter how you look at it, Rex Stewart will always hold a unique position in the history of jazz, although I am certain as I write these words that he will accuse me of gross exaggeration.